Far More Terrible
For Women

Other Titles in the Real Voices, Real History Series™

Far More Terrible For Women

Personal Accounts of Women in Slavery

Published by John F. Blair, Publisher

*The paper in this book meets the guidelines
for permanence and durability of the
Committee on Production Guidelines for
Book Longevity of the Council on Library Resources.*

Cover Image
Mary Reynolds, ca. 1936-1938
Courtesy of The Library of Congress, Manuscript Division

Library of Congress Cataloging-in-Publication Data

Far more terrible for women : personal accounts of women in slavery / edited by Patrick Minges.
    p.   cm. — (Real voices, real history series)
Includes bibliographical references.
ISBN-13: 978-0-89587-323-1 (alk. paper)
ISBN-10: 0-89587-323-0
1. Women slaves—Southern States—Interviews. 2. African American women—Southern
States—Interviews. 3. Women slaves—Southern States—Social conditions—19th century—
Anecdotes. 4. Slaves—Southern States—Social conditions—19th century—Anecdotes. 5.
Slavery—Southern States—History—19th century—Anecdotes. 6. Plantation life—Southern
States—History—19th century—Anecdotes. 7. Southern States—Race relations—History—
19th century—Anecdotes. 8. Interviews—Southern States. I. Minges, Patrick N. (Patrick
Neal), 1954-
 E444.F25 2006
 306.3'620820975—dc22
 [B]

2006019885

*Design by Debra Long Hampton
Composition by John Tarleton*

To Marion Szulkowski Payler, whose courage and strength of character reflect the women of this work

Contents

Introduction

"When they told me my new-born babe was a girl, my heart was heavier than it had ever been before. Slavery is terrible for men; but it is far more terrible for women. Superadded to the burden common to all, they have wrongs, and sufferings, and mortifications peculiarly their own."[1]

What do we know about the life of women under the "peculiar institution" of slavery as it was practiced in the United States in the nineteenth century?

Much of what we know comes from popular culture in the form of novels such as Toni Morrison's *Beloved*, Margaret Walker's *Jubilee*, Sherley Anne Williams's *Dessa Rose*, and Octavia Butler's *Kindred* and movies such as Jonathan Demme's *Beloved*, John Korty's *Autobiography of Miss Jane Pittman*, Julie Dash's *Daughters of the Dust*, and Haile Germina's *Sankofa*. Some may even know of slave life from the fictional portrayals of another era, such as *Gone With the Wind* and *Birth of a Nation*, which render shallow pastels of the rich and complex lives of women under the institution of slavery. We have come to understand this generation of women through the words of others, some sympathetic and others inclined to distort and discriminate.

Seldom, though, do we come to know of their struggle for dignity from the words of the women themselves. Some of the best resources for understanding the women who persevered the barbarity and dehumanization of slavery are the slave narratives of the nineteenth century and the ex-slave accounts found in the WPA narratives. As historian Deborah Gray White notes in her groundbreaking work, *Ar'n't I a Woman: Female Slaves in the Plantation South*, the narratives are "the richest, indeed almost the only black female source dealing with female slavery."[2] Saidiya Hartman, another researcher on the slave narratives, also believes in the value of these resources in understanding our collective history: "These narratives nonetheless remain an important source for understanding the everyday experience of slavery and its aftermath. . . . I read these documents with the hope of gaining a glimpse of black life during slavery and the postbellum period while remaining aware of the impossibility of fully reconstituting the experience of the enslaved."[3]

The history of women's slave narratives parallels the history of slavery, if not the history of the United States itself. Perhaps the earliest woman's slaves narrative comes from Isaiah Thomas's *Eccentric Biography: or, Memoirs of Remarkable Female Characters*, published in 1804. On pages 9 to 11 is the story of the slave Alice, whose parents had come from Barbados. Alice was born in Philadelphia around 1686 and died, still enslaved, in Bristol, Pennsylvania, in 1802. Though a slave, Alice was a ferry woman and, as such, she was unusually resourceful and independent. She witnessed the founding of Philadelphia and remembered its founder, William Penn. She also witnessed the founding of the African Methodist Episcopal

Church in Philadelphia.[4] In 1783, a slave by the name of Belinda petitioned a Massachusetts court for an allowance from her owner, who had abandoned her following the Revolutionary War. Her petition contained a narrative describing her capture in Africa and her transportation during the middle passage. She portrayed herself as a person bent "under the oppression of years" who was denied even one "morsel of that immense wealth . . . augmented by her servitude."[5] Some writers have posited that Belinda's petition was transcribed and published by poet Phyllis Wheatley or abolitionist Prince Hall, thus establishing a precedent that would become a characteristic of slave narratives in the nineteenth century.

It was in the nineteenth century—specifically, the period between 1830 and 1860, when the country was torn by sectional strife and the struggle over slavery—that the greatest number of women's slave narratives were published. Some became classics of the genre. Beginning with the *History of Mary Prince*, published in London in 1831, the slave narrative became an important part of the abolitionist struggle by highlighting the plight of captured Africans in their own words; Mary Prince's story was "supplied at trade price to Anti-Slavery Associations."[6] In 1850, *The Narrative of Sojourner Truth, a Northern Slave, Emancipated from Bodily Servitude by the State of New York, in 1828* was published "for the author" in Boston with the intent that "the perusal of the following Narrative may increase the sympathy that is felt for the suffering colored population of this country, and inspire renewed efforts for the liberation of all who are pining in bondage on the American soil."[7]

In 1853, a slave from North Carolina by the name of Harriet Jacobs began to publish her story in a different manner by sending several anonymous letters to the *New York Tribune*. With the support of antislavery activists, a collection of her stories was published as *Incidents in the Life of a Slave Girl* in Boston in 1860 and as *The Deeper Wrong; Or, Incidents in the Life of a Slave Girl* in London the following year. Upon the publication of *Incidents in the Life of a Slave Girl*, one of the most powerful dynamics of the master-slave relationship was laid open for all the world to see. On the very title page, she intimates what is to come: "Northerners know nothing at all about Slavery. They think it is perpetual bondage only. They have no conception of the depth of *degradation* involved in that word, *slavery*; if they had, they would never cease their efforts until so horrible a system was overthrown."[8] In the chapter entitled "The Trials of Girlhood," Jacobs reveals her intent to write "an expose of slavery as the violation of woman's nature":[9]

He tried his utmost to corrupt the pure principles my grandmother had instilled. He peopled my young mind with unclean images, such as only a vile monster could think of. I turned from him with disgust and hatred. But he was my master. I was compelled to live under the same roof with him—where I saw a man forty years my senior daily violating the most sacred commandments of nature. He told me I was his property; that I must be subject to his will in all things. My soul revolted against the mean tyranny. But where could I turn for protection? No matter whether the slave girl be as black as ebony or as fair as her mistress. In either case, there is no shadow of law to protect her from insult, from violence, or even from death; all these are inflicted by fiends who bear the shape of men. The mistress, who ought to protect the helpless victim, has no other feelings towards her but those of jealousy and rage. The degradation, the wrongs, the vices, that grow out of slavery, are more than I can describe. They are greater than you would willingly believe.[10]

With remarkable poignancy and prescience, she further articulates the troubled relationships between Southern sisters who shared the same gender yet lived across an unfathomable racial divide:

> I once saw two beautiful children playing together. One was a fair white child; the other was her slave, and also her sister. When I saw them embracing each other, and heard their joyous laughter, I turned sadly away from the lovely sight. I foresaw the inevitable blight that would fall on the little slave's heart. I knew how soon her laughter would be changed to sighs. The fair child grew up to be a still fairer woman. From childhood to womanhood her pathway was blooming with flowers, and overarched by a sunny sky. Scarcely one day of her life had been clouded when the sun rose on her happy bridal morning. How had those years dealt with her slave sister, the little playmate of her childhood? She, also, was very beautiful; but the flowers and sunshine of love were not for her. She drank the cup of sin, and shame, and misery, whereof her persecuted race are compelled to drink.[11]

The life of Harriet Jacobs is very much the story of one who drank from "the cup of sin, and shame, and misery." Her narrative further explicates the difficulties she faced at the hands of her owners and the community. When the wife of her owner became suspicious of his relationship with Harriet, the owner built a small home for Harriet where he could pursue his intentions away from his wife's "jealousy and rage." Having asked to marry a free black man, and having been refused that request by her owner, Harriet devised a plan where she might "triumph over my tyrant in some small way." She entered into a relationship with an unmarried white lawyer and bore children by him. Even though this action infuriated her owner, he refused to sell her and even continued his sexual advances towards her. When she learned that her master intended to put her children to work on the plantation, Harriet fled and lived in a tiny crawlspace for seven years, emerging only at night for exercise. In 1842, Harriet fled north, where her children joined her. Finally, in 1852, her freedom was purchased, after which she lived "as free from the power of slaveholders as are the white people of the north; and though that, according to my ideas, is not saying a great deal, it is a vast improvement in *my* condition."[12]

Harriet Jacobs's struggle against her master and mistress serves as a paradigm for understanding the plight of women under slavery. We see her plight at the hands of a cruel master who held her not only in bondage but in terror; we come to understand the desperate struggle to keep her children free from the blight that would befall little slaves' hearts. We also learn the remarkable story of her freedom and how it proved the focal point of her life.

One of the most interesting and underexplored resources for understanding the daily lives of women under slavery is the series of interviews conducted in the late 1930s by the Works Progress Administration of President Franklin Delano Roosevelt. These interviews had their inspiration in a series of historical and anthropological research projects of the late 1920s at Prairie View State College of Texas, Fisk University in Tennessee, Southern University of Louisiana, and Kentucky State College, where researchers collected and shaped autobiographical accounts of former slaves.[13] From these initial forays into the world of ex-slaves, a small number of ex-slave narratives were sporadically collected in Alabama, Arkansas, Florida, Georgia, South Carolina, Texas, and Virginia by a single black employee of the Federal Writers' Project, without explicit direction or apparent recognition from Washington.[14] In 1936, a group of black employees of the Florida Writers' Project—which included Zora Neale Hurston—interviewed a significant number of ex-slaves as part of a folklore project. A few of these narratives were sent to Washington, where project directors realized their potential. Within a year, a formal process of collecting ex-slave narratives commenced throughout the South.

By the time they finished, the Federal Writers' Project interviewers had spoken with some twenty-three hundred ex-slaves from almost twenty states and collected a body of supplementary materials such as photographs, ads for runaway slaves, bills of sale, and other non-narrative materials. Although the interviews were conducted largely in 1937 and 1938, the Federal Writers' Project was not able to organize the interviews and bind them for publication until 1941, when *A Folk History of Slavery in the United States* was presented to the Library of Congress. Though many different works such as *The Negro in Virginia, Drums and Shadows*, and *Gumbo-Ya-Ya* used elements of the collections, it was not until 1945 that its existence was widely publicized for the first time by Benjamin Botkin in *Lay My Burden Down: A Folk History of Slavery*.[15] The entire collection was not published until 1972, when Greenwood Publishing Company released a seventeen-volume edition entitled *The American Slave: A Composite Autobiography*, edited by George P. Rawick; it has since become a forty-one-volume effort.

As the ex-slave narratives constitute the largest body of first-person narratives ever collected in this country, they are a tremendously valuable cultural resource. However, as a historical resource, they do have their limitations. Historian John Blassingame has noted that an uncritical use of the slave narratives "will lead inevitably to a simplistic and distorted view of the plantation as a paternalistic institution where the chief feature of life was mutual love and respect between masters and slaves."[16] Indeed, the problems with the ex-slave narratives as a historical resource are many. The greatest issue is that of representation, since the narratives cover less than two percent of the available population that could have been interviewed. There is also the issue of biased reflections in order to curry favor with prominent, often white, interviewers who might have been seen as government agents capable of influencing the interviewees' financial situations. There are also temporal problems, one being the time span between the reflection and the actual incidents reported on and the other being the interviewers' requests to describe "slave times" in the midst of the Great Depression. There are also questions regarding the interview format and the interviewers themselves. The interviews were completely structured and afforded little spontaneity, and the interviewers either engaged in creative writing or recorded profoundly reified racial caricatures, as directed by Washington, which wanted the interviewers to record "Negro dialect." Additionally, few, if any, of the interviewers had professional training in field study or qualitative methodology, and their results often reflected their lack of training. And perhaps the most significant factor of all was the racial chasm that often divided interviewers from interviewees. There is every reason to believe that interviewees told interviewers—occasionally direct descendants of their former masters—just what they wanted to hear, or at least related their stories under the terms that racial etiquette of the day demanded.

All of this said, there is still great value in the slave narratives, as they provide the only firsthand testimony regarding the institution of slavery from the point of view of the enslaved. Indeed, many scholars are now coming to realize that whatever the limitations the slave narratives have as a historical resource, they provide an anthropological and cultural resource that is of great value simply because of its uniqueness. John Sekora, in "Black Message/White Envelope: Genre, Authenticity, and Authority in the Antebellum Slave Narrative," writes that, ultimately, the slave narrative must be valued as a historical resource:

In moral terms the slave narrative and its heirs are the only history of American slavery we have. Outside the narrative, slavery for black Americans was a wordless, nameless, timeless time. It was time without history and time without imminence. Existence was reduced largely to the duration of the psychological present. Or at least, according to Peter Walker, this was the only sense of time slaveholders would tolerate. For slaveholders the only reliable texts were their own records; the only valid recollection, from their own memories. Whatever else may be said about it, the slave narrative changed that forever. It gave some means and measure of fixity in a life of flux, and in this sense to recall one's history is to renew it. The slave narrative as written life story encouraged a recollection that could be tested, corrected, replenished. Such recollection could then be united with other life stories to form a history, a time beyond personal memory, a time beyond slaveholders' power.[17]

Just as the slave narratives may be "the only history of American slavery we have," the stories of women in the narratives certainly must be, as Deborah Gray White contends, "the richest, indeed almost the only black female source dealing with female slavery."[18] Of the nearly twenty-five hundred ex-slave narratives in the WPA collection, nearly fifteen hundred—approximately two-thirds—are from women. These narratives cover nearly all of the Southern states, as well as Nebraska, Minnesota, Washington, and the District of Columbia. Within them are stories of heroic as well as tragic proportions. As Harriet Jacobs notes in her narrative, many people have no appreciation for the depth of degradation that women endured as slaves, as well as little conception of their ability to transcend their appalling circumstances and to find liberation in the quality of the lives they were able to build. One of the first notions to be shattered by the narratives is any sense of understanding of what these women's lives were like. The complexities of their lives and the multifaceted and interconnected networks of being and existence prevent easy categorization of what it meant to be a female slave.

One of the more interesting aspects of these women's narratives is that, more often than not, both the interviewer and interviewee were women. Many of the women came from the same locale and knew each other as descendants of the plantation community. It is also true that many of the recorders attempted to tell their versions of the stories and even created fanciful narratives in which their telling superseded their actual intent. Though this tendency is problematic and hardly good social science, it is fascinating in how it replicates the netherworld that existed between sisters of the South who stood on opposite sides of the racial hierarchy. What is equally fascinating is the way in which the interviewers attempt to tell the ex-slaves' stories in their own words, and the remarkable manner in which these stories take on a literary quality of their own. I have included some of these third-person stories because of the interesting insights they provide of the women who conducted the interviews and composed the narratives.

The more we try to understand these women, the more we find that our understanding is shaped by our own mythological and ideological presuppositions about them. The complicated issues of representation and interpretation plague us no less than they did the interviewers who recorded these women's life stories in the late 1930s. Whereas race was always a mitigating factor in transpersonal communication in the ex-slave narratives, we now have the compounding issues of race *and* gender. Whatever complexities are involved in these issues, we must work through them if we are to make sense of these women's experiences in order to find a common link between their lives and our own. Ultimately, everything that we know and do is built upon the political, social, and personal framework that these women helped establish. We are indebted to them for our very existence.

To compile this collection, I went through the body of the WPA ex-slave interviews in search of women's narratives. I collected these by state and reviewed them to find the most compelling stories. The selection was not based on any scholarly or ideological presuppositions and is not intended to put forward any; the narratives were selected solely because they relate issues relevant to women's experiences under slavery or because they are intriguing or provocative. In reviewing the narratives, I found some common themes and grouped the stories according to these themes—Jezebel and Mammy, Friends and Families, Witches/Doctors, Mother/Child, and Herstory.

I provide a brief introduction to each section of narratives touching on the contexts of the stories and information about the interviewees and in some cases the interviewers. Then come the narratives themselves. Each is preceded by the interviewee's name, some basic demographic information, and the source of the narrative.

I have made some adjustments to accommodate the narratives' varied styles and formats. When the narrative is told in the first person, when it is presented in the third person in the words of the interviewer, or when it is an integrated blend of the two, it will appear in regular type with the interviewee's words in quotation marks. But when the interviewer's comments serve as an overview of, or as an interruption to, the ex-slave's words, the interviewer's comments appear in italics. Comments in brackets are meant to clarify arcane meanings. I hope this will serve as a means to make the complex interactions between interviewers and interviewees more accessible.

These stories are presented not as a definitive model for understanding women's experiences under the institution of slavery but to facilitate dialogue around the issues so we can begin to collectively articulate some tentative sketches of that experience. In these stories are dramatic images of life and death, pain and perseverance, devastation and deliverance, all related by the women whose memories serve as a record and reflection of a turbulent period in American history. They speak of a time long gone but whose importance demands respect and reverence.

Jezebel and Mammy

"Big Jim would make them consummate this relationship in his presence. He used the same procedure if he thought a certain couple was not producing children fast enough. He enjoyed these orgies very much and often entertained his friends in this manner; quite often, he and his guests would engage in these debaucheries, choosing for themselves the prettiest of the young women. Sometimes, they forced the unhappy husbands and lovers of their victims to look on."

Louise Everett interview

Jezebel and Mammy

In the first chapter of her consummate work on women and slavery, *Ar'n't I a Woman: Female Slaves in the Plantation South*, Deborah Gray White posits that the prevailing mythology of enslaved women in the antebellum period consisted of an essential dualism; the enslaved female was either a "Jezebel" or a "Mammy." She describes the mythology thus: "Many Southerners were able to embrace both images of black women simultaneously and to switch from one to the other depending on the context of their thought. On the one hand there was the woman obsessed with matters of the flesh, on the other was the asexual woman. One was carnal, the other maternal. One was at heart a slut, the other was deeply religious. One was a Jezebel, the other a Mammy."[19]

These images, almost archetypal in their representation of female identity throughout history—Mary Magdalene and the Virgin Mary, for example—have served to perpetuate the subjugation of women within the political and social structure. Within the antebellum culture, these ideologies served as a justification for white sexual exploitation of enslaved women on one hand

and the ennobling aspect of domestic slavery on the other.[20] Unfortunately, these images carried beyond the antebellum period through the early twentieth century, when the WPA narratives were framed, and even into the modern period as the welfare queen and the matriarch.

The concept of black women as licentious arose when Europeans first encountered persons from traditional cultures for whom the tropical climate rendered some clothing unnecessary. Their misreading of all African cultural practices was fed by their own preconceived ideals about the distinctions between "civilized" nations and the indigenous "savages"; traditional marriages became examples of uncontrolled lust, sacred dance became a profane exhibition of limitless passion, and celebrations of the sacred ties to nature became pagan orgies. Carrying this one step further, vanity and prejudice combined to convince colonial patriarchs and their progeny that women of color desired sexual relations with white men. It is important to note that prejudicial gender conventions also applied to black men and served as a great threat to their existence. But the menace of sexual violence toward female slaves was ever present and ever powerful.

The women in the enslaved community, both celebrated and vilified in popular culture, often lived free of the societal restrictions of the Victorian era that limited the options of slaveholding women. This freedom, or even the perception of its existence, served to legitimize the gratuitous sexual advances of white men, who believed that enslaved women were possessed by desirous intent to be with their owners, and that the women's insatiable appetite for sex necessitated their ministrations. This pervasive opinion provided justification for sexual violence and also promoted the self-esteem of Southern men, who believed they had a certain social responsibility to quell the libidinous urges of their charges. That many female slaves were valued for their procreative capabilities and that such capabilities enriched the slaveholders' households further promoted the mythology that undergirded the Jezebel ideology.[21]

The contradistinction to Jezebel was the notion of the asexual, long-suffering, and devoted household assistant whose very nature defined the paternalistic and positive aspects of the "peculiar institution." Of all the ideologies that have been transmitted to the modern era from the antebellum period, the idealized image of "Mammy" is perhaps the most persistent and all-encompassing. The caricature remains with us in spite of the fact that it is perhaps the most mythologized of images and may exist only in our minds. "Records do acknowledge the presence of female slaves who served as the 'right hand' of plantation mistresses," writes Catherine Clinton in *The Plantation Mistress: Woman's World in the Old South.* "Yet documents from the planter class during the first fifty years following the American Revolution reveal only a handful of such examples. Not until after Emancipation did black women run white households or occupy in any significant number the special positions ascribed to them in folklore and fiction. The Mammy was created by white Southerners to redeem the relationship between black women and white men within slave society in response to the antislavery attack from the North during the ante-bellum period. In the primary records from before the Civil War, hard evidence for its existence simply does not appear."[22]

"Mammy" was therefore created to respond to the concern of Northern abolitionists over the sexual violence against enslaved women that was an omnipresent reality of antebellum life. Whereas the Jezebel was an erotic primal beauty possessed by her sensuality, the Mammy was the exact opposite. No slave owner would choose the matronly, desexualized, frivolous elder woman over his white wife. Thus, the household and, by extension, the institution of slavery were protected.

Mammy preserved the organic harmony of the slaveholding family unit and articulated a supposed positive nature of the institution of slavery. Whereas the reality of slavery was often resistance and hostility, the Mammy presented an image of nurture and devotion within a benevolent association. She preserved the social order within the enslaved community and the larger household and was a bulwark against structural change and social disorder. Because of her identity as a racial stereotype and her importance in the maintenance of racial order in Southern history, her image found expression in literary circles and popular culture into the twentieth century. As such, she helped frame many of the discussions within the WPA ex-slave narratives. The tenuous balance between Mammy and Jezebel found ample expression within the descriptions of these women's lives.

In his article in the *New York Times* celebrating the HBO series *Unchained Memories: Readings from the Slave Narratives*, Henry Louis Gates lifts up the story of Rose Williams from Texas, who discusses her forced marriage to another slave, "an institutionalized form of rape commonly practiced on the plantation."[23] Rosa is placed first in this section not just for the story of her forced marriage but because her owner was a "nigger trader." Her time on the block recapitulates everything negative that we have come to understand about the Jezebel notion. With her parents already sold, she is presented on the block as a "portly, strong wench" who has never been abused and who "will make a good breeder." In spite of this, she sweats out her time on the block before she is finally bought by her parents' new owner. Though her new master does not treat her harshly, she can never forgive him, nor does she ever marry after he "force me to live with dat nigger Rufus 'gainst my wants."

Louisa Everett's story bespeaks the degradation of humanity that belied any attempts of the Southern aristocracy to paint a pleasant face on women in the enslaved community. Her owner regularly beat his slaves and hung them by their thumbs for no reason at all. He forced slaves to procreate against their will, and if they resisted, he made them do it in his presence. Pregnant mothers worked in the fields even unto the delivery of their children. The sick were forced to work, and there was never time for play. "Big Jim" regularly had "orgies," taking advantage of the women on his plantation and allowing his friends to do the same; he often forced the partners of the women to watch as he and his friends engaged in their debaucheries. Though some marriages were festive affairs, Louisa's description of her "courtship" and marriage is a sad tale indeed, and one that will not soon slip from the mind.

The story of Leah Garrett shows the extent to which an ill-treated slave would go to escape her abuser and how both her husband and her community would hide her. It also shows the litany of torture devices used to discipline slaves and the consequences upon both the individual slaves and the community at large. Her story provides a glimpse into the heart of one who placed a slave in a torture device even though the "poor thing already had heart trouble" and then calmly "went to church, preached, and called hisself servin' God." This God-fearing tyrant would allow his slaves to worship, too, but "dey always had somebody to follow de slaves to church when de colored preacher was preachin' to hear what was said and done. Dey was 'fraid us would try to say something 'gainst 'em." Such was the life of Leah Garrett.

The stories of the Mammies begin with that of Rena Clark, whose tale is told, ironically, in the third person. Her narrative comes from Lafayette County, Mississippi, between the Tallahatchie River and the Yoknapatawpha River, which served as the prototype for William Faulkner's fictional Yoknapatawpha County. Faulkner lived in Oxford, the county seat of Lafayette County; nearly all his work is set in this locale. If there is a proto-typical caricature within this collection, it is certainly the story of Rena Clark. And if ever the racial stereotypes and racist frame-work of the 1930s South are apparent, it is in this narrative. The interviewer refers to Rena several times as a "darkie" and reports, almost with incredulity, that she "calls herself an 'herb doctor.' " This narrative shows the problems inherent in using the ex-slave narratives as a source for historical research but at the same time provides a fascinating glimpse of how the Mammy ideology persevered.

A lengthy introduction is provided by the interviewer of Aunt Betty Cofer from near Winston-Salem, North Carolina. The ex-slave of Dr. Beverly Jones, whose family owned a fifteen-hundred-acre plot near Bethania for several generations, she presents herself with an "innate dignity, gentle courtesy, and complete self-possession [that] indicate long association with 'quality folks.' " "Claimed" at a very young age by one of the Jones daughters, Aunt Betty "most times slept on the floor in her room." Her mother was a cook for the Joneses. Although Betty Cofer was a landowner and a distinguished member of her community, the interviewer sees her as "still at heart a 'Jones Negro,' and all the distinguished descendants of her beloved Marse Beverly and Miss Julia will be her 'own folks' as long as she lives."

The last story in this section is one of the most interesting of all. Though contained within the ex-slave narratives, it is not the recollections of an ex-slave at all but those of an ex-slave owner, Mrs. Betty Quesnesberry of Arkansas. The first indication that things are different in this tale comes when the interviewer notes that "over the fireplace hangs an oil painting three feet square which is more than one hundred years old. This is the picture of her grandfather, who was a big slaveholder in Virginia." Things get even more curious as the interviewer relates Bible stories told to Mrs. Quesnesberry by her slave caretaker and describes the "bond between this child, Betty Greene, who is now Mrs. Quesnesberry, and her Negro 'Mammy.' " Perhaps the most interesting aspect of this story of slavery not told by a slave is that all of the questions that would have been asked of a slave are asked of Mrs. Quesnesberry, and she relates all that she can remember of the slavery experience.

ROSE WILLIAMS

Born: 1846
Age: Ninety
Master: Hall Hawkins
Place: Bell County, Texas
Interviewer: Sheldon Gauthier
Source: Second Supplemental Series, Texas Narratives,
   volume 10T, page 4117

Rose Williams, ninety, was born a slave to Mr. William Black, a slave trader who owned many slaves in addition to Rose's parents and a plantation in Bell County, Texas. Rose was about fifteen years old at the start of the Civil War when she and her parents with about ten other slaves were sold in a public auction to Mr. Hall Hawkins. Mr. Hawkins owned a plantation with about fifty slaves in Bell County, Texas. The buying and selling of slaves and the mating of the largest slaves being an ordinary function on the plantations, Rose was forced to mate and live with another slave when she was but sixteen years old. She made him leave after her freedom. She had two children by him, one of them born after freedom. This early domestic experience created in her an antipathy against marriage which she retained the rest of her life, and she has never married. She worked as a farm laborer until about thirty years ago, when she moved to Fort Worth. She has been blind and unable to work the past ten years. She now resides at 1126 Hapton Street, Fort Worth, Texas. Her story:

"What I say am de facts. If I's one day old, I's way over ninety, and I's born in Bell County, right here in Texas, and am owned by Massa William Black. He owns Mammy and Pappy, too. Massa Black has a big plantation, but he has more niggers dan he need for work on dat place, 'cause he am a nigger trader. He trade and buy and sell all de time.

"Massa Black am awful cruel, and he whip de cullud folks and works 'em hard and feed 'em poorly. We-uns have for rations de cornmeal and milk and 'lasses and some beans and peas, and meat once a week. We-uns have to work in de field every day from daylight till dark, and on Sunday we-uns do us washin'. Church? Shucks, we-uns don't know what dat mean.

"I has de clearest memorandum of when de war start.

"Massa Black sold we-uns right den. Mammy and Pappy powerful glad to get sold, and dey and I is put on de block with 'bout ten other niggers. When we-uns gets to de tradin' block, dere lots of white folks dere what come to look us over. One man shows de interest in Pappy. Him named Hawkins. He talk to Pappy, and Pappy talk to him and say, 'Dem my woman and chiles. Please buy all of us and have mercy on we-uns.' Massa Hawkins say, 'Dat gal am a likely lookin' nigger, she am portly and strong, but three am more dan I wants, I guesses.'

"De sale start, and 'fore long, Pappy am put on de block. Massa Hawkins wins de bid for Pappy, and when Mammy am put on de block, he wins de bid for her. Den dere am three or four other niggers sold before my time comes. Den Massa Black calls me to de block, and de auction man say, 'What am I offer for dis portly, strong wench? She's never been 'bused and will make a good breeder.'

"I wants to hear Massa Hawkins bid, but him say nothin'. Two other men am biddin' against each other, and I sho has de worriment. Dere am tears comin' down my cheeks 'cause I's bein' sold to some man dat would make separation from my mammy. One man bids five hundred dollars, and de auction man ask, 'Do I hear more? She am gwine at five hundred dollars.' Den someone say, 'Five hundred twenty-five,' and de auction man say, 'She am sold for five hundred twenty-five dollars to Massa Hawkins.' Am I glad and 'cited! Why, I's quiverin' all over.

"Massa Hawkins takes we-uns to his place, and it am a nice plantation. Lots better am dat place dan Massa Black's. Dere is 'bout fifty niggers what is growed and lots of chillun. De first thing Massa do when we-uns gets home am give we-uns rations and a cabin. You must believe dis nigger when I says dem rations was a feast for us. Dere was plenty meat and tea and coffee and white flour. I's never tasted white flour and coffee, and Mammy fix some biscuits and coffee. Well, de biscuits was yum-yum to me, but de coffee I doesn't like.

"De quarters am pretty good. Dere am twelve cabins all made from logs, and a table and some benches, and bunks for sleepin', and a fireplace for cookin' and de heat. Dere am no floor, just de ground.

"Massa Hawkins am good to he niggers and not force 'em too hard. Dere am as much difference 'tween him and old Massa Black in de way of treatment as 'twixt de Lawd and de devil. Massa Hawkins 'lows de niggers to have reasonable parties and go fishin', but we-uns am never taken to church and has no books for learnin'. Dere am no education for de niggers.

"Dere am one thing Massa Hawkins does to me what I can't shunt from my mind. I knows he don't do it for meanness, but I allus holds it 'gainst him. What he done am force me to live with dat nigger Rufus 'gainst my wants.

"After I been at he place 'bout a year, de massa come to me and say, 'You gwine live with Rufus in dat cabin over yonder. Go fix it for livin'.' I's 'bout sixteen year old and has no learnin', and I's just a ignoramus chile. I's thought dat him mean for me to tend de cabin for Rufus and some other niggers. Well, dat am de start of de pestigation for me.

"I's took charge of de cabin after work am done and fixes supper. Now, I don't like Rufus 'cause he a bully. He am big, and 'cause he so he think everybody do what him say. We-uns has supper, den I goes here and dere talkin' till I's ready for sleep, and den I gets in de bunk. After I's in, dat nigger come and crawl in de bunk with me 'fore I knows it. I says, 'What you means, you fool nigger?' He say for me to hush de mouth. 'Dis am my bunk, too,' he say. 'You's teched in de head. Get out,' I's told him, and I puts de feet against him and give him a shove, and out he go on de floor 'fore he know what I's doin'. Dat nigger jump up, and he mad. He look like de wild bear. He starts for de bunk, and I jumps quick for de poker. It am 'bout three feet long, and when he comes at me I lets him have it over de head. Did dat nigger stop in he tracks? I's say he did. He looks at me steady for a minute, and you could tell he thinkin' hard. Den he go and set on de bench and say, 'Just wait. You thinks you am smart, but you am foolish in de head. Dey's gwine learn you somethin'.' 'Hush you big mouth and stay away from dis nigger, dat all I wants,' I say, and I just sets and hold dat poker in de hand. He just sets, lookin' like de bull. Dere we-uns sets and sets for 'bout an hour, and den he go out and I bars de door.

"De next day, I goes to de missy and tells her what Rufus wants, and de missy say dat am de massa's wishes. She say, 'You am de portly gal, and Rufus am de portly man. De massa wants you-uns for to bring forth portly chillun.' I's thinkin' 'bout what de missy say, but say to myself, 'I's not gwine live with dat Rufus.'

"Dat night when him come in de cabin, I grabs de poker and sets on de bench and says, 'Get from me, nigger, 'fore I busts you brains out and stomp on 'em.' He says nothin' and get out.

"De next day, de massa call me and tell me, 'Woman, I's pay big money for you, and I's done dat 'cause I wants you to raise me chillun. I's put you to live with Rufus for dat purpose. Now, if you doesn't want whippin' at de stake, you do what I wants.'

"I thinks 'bout Massa buyin' me off de block and savin' me from bein' separated from my folks, and 'bout bein' whipped at de stake. Dere it am. What am I to do? I decides to do as de massa wish, and so I yields.

"When we-uns am given freedom, Massa Hawkins tells us we can stay and work for wages or sharecrop de land. Some stays and some goes. My folks and me stays. We works de land on shares for three years, den moves to other land nearby. I stays with my folks till they dies.

"If my memorandum am correct, it am 'bout thirty year since I come to Fort Worth. Here, I cooks for white folks till I goes blind 'bout ten year ago.

"I never marries 'cause one experience am nuff for dis nigger. After what I does for de massa, I's never want no truck with any man. De Lawd forgive dis colored woman, but he have to 'scuse me and look for some others for to 'plenish de earth."

LOUISA EVERETT

Born: 1847
Age: Ninety
Master: Jim McClain
Place: Virginia
Interviewer: Pearl Randolph
Source: First Series, Library of Congress Rare Book Room
   Collection, Florida Narratives, volume 17A, page 126

Sam and Louise Everett, eighty-six and ninety years of age, respectively, have weathered together some of the worst experiences of slavery, and as they look back over the years can relate these experiences as clearly as if they had happened only yesterday.

Both were born near Norfolk, Virginia, and were sold as slaves several times on nearby plantations. It was on the plantation of Big Jim McClain that they met as slave children and departed after emancipation to live the lives of free people.

Sam was the son of Peter and Betsy Everett, field hands who spent long, backbreaking hours in the cotton fields and came home at nightfall to cultivate their small garden. They lived in constant fear that their master would confiscate most of their vegetables; he so often did.

Louisa remembers little about her parents and thinks that she was sold at an early age to a separate master. Her name as nearly as she could remember was Norfolk Virginia. Everyone called her "Nor." It was not until after she was freed and had sent her children to school that she changed her name to Louisa.

Sam and Norfolk spent part of their childhood on the plantation of Big Jim, who was very cruel; often, he would whip his slaves into insensibility for minor offenses. He sometimes hung them up by their thumbs whenever they were caught attempting to escape—"er fer no reason at all."

On this plantation were more than a hundred slaves, who were mated indiscriminately and without any regard for family unions. If their master thought that a certain man and woman might have strong, healthy offspring, he forced them to have sexual relations, even though they were married to other slaves. If there seemed to be any slight reluctance on the part of either of the unfortunate ones, Big Jim would make them consummate this relationship in his presence. He used the same procedure if he thought a certain couple was not producing children fast enough. He enjoyed these orgies very much and often entertained his friends in this manner; quite often, he and his guests would engage in these debaucheries, choosing for themselves the prettiest of the young women. Sometimes, they forced the unhappy husbands and lovers of their victims to look on.

Louisa and Sam were married in a very revolting manner. To quote the woman:

"Marse Jim called me and Sam ter him and ordered Sam to pull off his shirt—that was all the McClain niggers wore—and he said to me, 'Nor, do you think you can stand this big nigger?' He had that old bullwhip flung across his shoulder, and Lawd, that man could hit so hard! So I just said, 'Yessir, I guess so,' and tried to hide my face so I couldn't see Sam's nakedness, but he made me look at him anyhow.

"Well, he told us we must get busy and do it in his presence, and we had to do it. After that, we were considered man and wife. Me and Sam was a healthy pair and had fine, big babies, so I never had another man forced on me, thank God. Sam was kind to me, and I learnt to love him."

Life on the McClain plantation was a steady grind of work from morning until night. Slaves had to rise in the dark of the morning at the ringing of the big-house bell. After eating a hasty breakfast of fried fat pork and corn pone, they worked in the fields until the bell rang again at noon, at which time they ate boiled vegetables, roasted sweet potatoes, and black molasses. This food was cooked in iron pots which had legs attached to their bottoms in order to keep them from resting directly on the fire. These utensils were either hung over a fire or set atop a mound of hot coals. Biscuits were a luxury, but whenever they had white bread it was cooked in another thick pan called a "spider." This pan had a top which was covered with hot embers to ensure the browning of the bread on top.

Slave women had no time for their children. These were cared for by an old woman who called them twice a day and fed them "pot likker" (vegetable broth) and skimmed milk. Each child was provided with a wooden ladle, which he dipped into a wooden trough and fed himself. The older children fed those who were too young to hold a ladle.

So exacting was Big Jim that slaves were forced to work even when sick. Expectant mothers toiled in the fields until they felt their labor pains. It was not uncommon for babies to be born in the fields.

There was little time for play on his plantation. Even the very small children were assigned tasks. They hunted hens' eggs, gathered pokeberries for dyeing, shelled corn, and drove the cows home in the evening. Little girls knitted stockings.

There was no church on this plantation, and itinerant ministers avoided going there because of the owner's cruelty. Very seldom were the slaves allowed to attend neighboring churches, and still rarer were the opportunities to hold meetings among themselves. Often when they were in the middle of a song or prayer, they would be forced to halt and run to the big house. Woe to any slave who ignored the ringing of the bell that summoned him to work and told him when he might "knock off" from his labors.

Louisa and Sam last heard the ringing of this bell in the fall of 1865. All the slaves gathered in front of the big house to be told that they were free for the time being. They had heard whisperings of the war but did not understand the meaning of it all. Now, Big Jim stood weeping on the piazza and cursing the fate that had been so cruel to him by robbing him of all his "niggers." He inquired if any wanted to remain until all the crops were harvested, and when no one consented to do so he flew into a rage. Seizing his pistol, he began firing into the crowd of frightened Negroes. Some were killed outright, and others were maimed for life. Finally, he was prevailed upon to stop. He then attempted to take his own life. A few frightened slaves promised to remain with him another year; this placated him. It was necessary for Union soldiers to make another visit to the plantation before Big Jim would allow his former slaves to depart.

Sam and Louisa moved to Boston, Georgia, where they sharecropped for several years. They later bought a small farm when their two sons became old enough to help. They continued to live on this homestead until a few years ago, when their advancing ages made it necessary that they live with the children. Both of the children had settled in Florida several years previous and wanted their parents to come to them. They now live in Mulberry, Florida, with the younger son. Both are pitifully infirm but can still remember the horrors they experienced under very cruel owners. It was with difficulty that they were prevailed upon to relate some of the gruesome details recorded here.

LEAH GARRETT

Born: Unknown
Age: Unknown
Master: Unknown
Place: Unknown
Interviewer: Unknown
Source: First Series, Library of Congress Rare Book Room
    Collection, Georgia Narratives, volume 12B, page 11

Leah Garrett, an old Negress with snow-white hair, leaned back in her rocker and recalled customs and manners of slavery days. Mistreatment at the hands of her master is outstanding in her memory.

"I know so many things 'bout slavery time till I never will be able to tell 'em all. In dem days, preachers was just as bad and mean as anybody else. Dere was a man who folks called a good preacher, but he was one of de meanest mens I ever seed. When I was in slavery under him, he done so many bad things till God soon kilt him. His wife or chillun could get mad wid you, and if dey told him anything he always beat you. Most times, he beat his slaves when dey hadn't done nothin' at all.

One Sunday mornin', his wife told him their cook wouldn't never fix nothin' she told her to fix. Time she said it, he jumped up from de table, went in de kitchen, and made de cook go under de porch where he always whupped his slaves. She begged and prayed, but he didn't pay no 'tention to dat. He put her up in what us called de swing and beat her till she couldn't holler. De poor thing already had heart trouble—dat's why he put her in de kitchen—but he left her swingin' there and went to church, preached, and called hisself servin' God. When he got back home, she was dead. Whenever your marster had you swingin' up, nobody wouldn't take you down. Sometimes a man would help his wife, but most times he was beat afterwards.

"Another marster I had kept a hogshead to whup you on. Dis hogshead had two or three hoops round it. He buckled you face down on de hogshead and whupped you till you bled. Everybody always stripped you in dem days to whup you 'cause dey didn't care who seed you naked. Some folks' chillun took sticks and jobbed [jabbed] you all while you was bein' beat. Sometimes, dese chillun would beat you all 'cross your head, and dey mas and pas didn't know what *stop* was.

"Another way Marster had to whup us was in a stock dat he had in de stables. Dis was where he whupped you when he was real mad. He had logs fixed together wid holes for your feet, hands, and head. He had a way to open dese logs and fasten you in. Then he had his coachman give you so many lashes, and he would let you stay in de stock for so many days and nights. Dat's why he had it in de stable, so it wouldn't rain on you. Every day, you got dat same number of lashes. You never come out able to sit down.

"I had a cousin wid two chillun. De oldest one had to nurse one of Marster's grandchildren. De front steps was real high, and one day dis poor chile fell down dese steps wid de baby.

His wife and daughter hollered and went on terrible, and when our marster come home dey was still hollerin' just like de baby was dead or dyin'. When dey told him 'bout it, he picked up a board and hit dis poor little chile 'cross de head and kilt her right there. Then he told his slaves to take her and throw her in de river. Her ma begged and prayed, but he didn't pay her no 'tention; he made 'em throw de chile in.

"One of de slaves married a young gal, and dey put her in de big house to work. One day, Mistress jumped on her 'bout something, and de gal hit her back. Mistress said she was goin' to have Marster put her in de stock and beat her when he come home. When de gal went to de field and told her husband 'bout it, he told her where to go and stay till he got there. Dat night, he took his supper to her. He carried her to a cave and hauled pine straw and put it in there for her to sleep on. He fixed dat cave up just like a house for her, put a stove in there and run de pipe out through de ground into a swamp. Everybody always wondered how he fixed dat pipe. Course, dey didn't cook on it till night, when nobody could see de smoke. He sealed de house wid pine logs, made beds and tables out of pine poles, and dey lived in dis cave seven years. Durin' dis time, dey had three chillun. Nobody was wid her when dese chillun was born but her husband. He waited on her wid each chile. De chillun didn't wear no clothes 'cept a piece tied round their waists. Dey was just as hairy as wild people, and dey was wild. When dey come out of dat cave, dey would run every time dey seed a person.

"De seven years she lived in de cave, different folks helped keep 'em in food. Her husband would take it to a certain place, and she would go and get it. People had passed over dis cave ever so many times, but nobody knowed dese folks was livin' there. Our marster didn't know where she was, and it was freedom 'fore she come out of dat cave for good.

"Us lived in a long house dat had a flat top and little rooms made like mule stalls, just big enough for you to get in and sleep. Dey weren't no floors in dese rooms and neither no beds. Us made beds out of dry grass, but us had cover 'cause de real old people who couldn't do nothin' else made plenty of it. Nobody weren't 'lowed to have fires, and if dey was caught wid any dat meant a beatin'. Some would burn charcoal and take de coals to their rooms to help warm 'em.

"Every person had a tin pan, tin cup, and a spoon. Everybody couldn't eat at one time; us had 'bout four different sets. Nobody had a stove to cook on. Everybody cooked on fireplaces and used skillets and pots. To boil, us hung pots on racks over de fire and baked bread and meats in de skillets.

"Marster had a big room right 'side his house where his vittles was cooked. Then de cook had to carry 'em upstairs in a tray to be served. When de somethin' to eat was carried to de dinin' room, it was put on a table and served from dis table. De food weren't put on de eatin' table.

"De slaves went to church wid dey marsters. De preachers always preached to de white folks first, den dey would preach to de slaves. Dey never said nothin' but 'You must be good, don't steal, don't talk back at your marsters, don't run away, don't do dis, and don't do dat.' Dey let de colored preachers preach, but dey give 'em almanacs to preach out of. Dey didn't 'low us to sing such songs as 'We Shall Be Free' and 'O For a Thousand Tongues to Sing.' Dey always had somebody to follow de slaves to church when de colored preacher was preachin' to hear what was said and done. Dey was 'fraid us would try to say something 'gainst 'em."

RENA CLARK

Born: 1849
Age: Eighty-seven
Master: Nick Pegues
Place: Lafayette County, Mississippi
Interviewer: Ruth Price
Source: First Supplemental Series, Mississippi Narratives,
    volume 07S, page 408

Rena Clark, an old "black mammy" who says she is eighty-seven years old but really looks much older, came to this country with the "Mr. Nick Pegues family" when she was two years old. "Aunt Rena," almost blind now, is very religious. She has always read the Bible all of her spare time ever since Miss Rebecca Pegues taught her to read when she was twelve years old, until she lost her eyesight a few years ago. Even though her poor old eyes are sightless now and she can no longer read the "blessed book," it lives on in her heart, and she quotes many passages of scripture from memory. She is a genial, kind old soul who loves her fellow man. This is a mighty fine religion for black or white, it seems.

One remarkable thing about Rena is that even though she is nearly ninety years old, she has never lost a tooth and says she has never had the toothache in her life. She smokes a corn-cob pipe, and she thinks this has preserved her teeth.

Rena has always been a wealthy white folks' darkie, which makes her circumstances seem very pitiful now. At present, she is dependent upon her daughter, who looks almost as old as she herself. There are four generations of them living in a little two-room cabin down in Negro Hollow. This morning, her daughter, Carrie, was washing on the front porch and hanging clothes on a line in the front yard, and her little great-grand-child, Lulie, was pulling up weeds in a flower bed by the doorstep. Lulie's mother, Lillie, has a job cooking for some white folks.

Rena says she has acted as midwife ever since she was fif-teen years old and has "done brought a passel" of babies into this world. She says she has attended both white and colored for over fifty years. The first thing when a baby is born, Rena says, she would bathe and dress him and then she would tie a mole's right foot around his neck. This was to keep him in good health and to bring him good luck. No conscientious "black mammy" would neglect this charm. When Rena's babies began teething, she always tied six small white buttons around their necks along with the mole's foot. If this was done, a child would never feel any pain and would not know he was cutting teeth. If he should have colic, Rena's remedy was a mixture of sugar and soot from the tenth brick in the chimney. Rena says when a baby is six months old, he ought to have the hives. If he failed to break out with them, the best thing to do would be to give him a dose of warm catnip tea. To keep away such diseases as measles, mumps, whooping cough, etc., Rena says she always tied on a little bag of asafetida, this also around his neck. On being asked if she didn't think this was a good deal to tie around the neck of one baby, she said, "No, ma'am, you'd better do dis dan let 'em die without no 'tention."

Rena calls herself an "herb doctor." She says she can cure most everything that ails the womenfolks. When asked, "How about the men?" she said, "I don't fool wid doctoring no mens. I don't know nothin' about dere ailments. It always looked like dey could take care of deyselves anyhow. I just doctors women troubles."

Rena, on being asked how darkies were married before the war, said, "Dey just jumped over de broomstick, and some of 'em didn't have dat much ceremony." Rena's white folks, however, believed in doing things right, and she was married by a white preacher.

When asked about funeral wakes, she said she didn't know anything about wakes, but colored folks always "set up" with their "daid." They have, she says, "songs, prayers, and mournin' all night." According to Rena, all the kinfolks and friends come and take part in this "set up." Sometimes during the night, they cook and eat. She goes on to tell how, when a colored person dies, the pictures in the room are covered up and the mirrors turned to the wall; also, the clocks are always stopped in the room. On being asked why the clocks are stopped, she said she reckoned it was so niggers could hear noises around the house, that they didn't want no haints slipping up on them.

Rena strongly disapproves of the young colored people of this day and generation. She says, "They don't have the proper respect for funerals no mo'."

AUNT BETTY COFER

Born: 1856
Age: Eighty-one
Master: Dr. Beverly Jones
Place: Wachovia area, North Carolina
Interviewer: Mary E. Hicks
Source: First Series, Library of Congress Rare Book Room
    Collection, North Carolina Narratives, volume 14A,
    page 163

The ranks of Negro ex-slaves are rapidly thinning out, but scattered here and there among the antebellum families of the South may be found a few of these picturesque old characters. Three miles north of Bethania, the second-oldest settlement of the "Unitas Fratrum" in Wachovia, lies the fifteen-hundred-acre Jones plantation. It has been owned for several generations by one family, descendants of Abraham Conrad. Conrad's daughter, Julia, married a physician of note, Dr. Beverly Jones, whose family occupied the old homestead at the time of the Civil War.

Here, in 1856, was born a Negro girl, Betty, to a slave mother. Here, today, under the friendly protection of this same Jones family, surrounded by her sons and her sons' sons, lives this same Betty in her own little weather-stained cottage. Encircling her house are lilacs, althea, and flowering trees that soften the bleak outlines of unpainted outbuildings. A varied collection of old-fashioned plants and flowers crowds the neatly swept dooryard. A friendly German shepherd puppy rouses from his nap on the sunny porch to greet visitors enthusiastically. In answer to our knock, a gentle voice calls, "Come in." The door opens directly into a small, low-ceilinged room almost filled by two double beds. These beds are conspicuously clean and covered by homemade crocheted spreads. Wide bands of handmade insertions ornament the stiffly starched pillow slips. Against the wall is a plain oak dresser. Although the day is warm, two-foot logs burn on the age-worn andirons of the wide brick fireplace. From the shelf above dangles a leather bag of "spills" made from twisted newspapers.

In a low, split-bottom chair, her rheumatic old feet resting on the warm brick hearth, sits Aunt Betty Cofer. Her frail body stoops under the weight of four score years, but her bright eyes and alert mind are those of a woman thirty years younger. A blue-checked mobcap covers her grizzled hair. Her tiny frame, clothed in a motley collection of undergarments, dress, and sweaters, is adorned by a clean white apron. Although she is a little shy of her strange white visitors, her innate dignity, gentle courtesy, and complete self-possession indicate long association with "quality folks."

Her speech shows a noticeable freedom from the usual heavy Negro dialect and idiom of the Deep South.

"Yes, ma'am, yes, sir, come in. Pull a chair to the fire. You'll have to 'scuse me. I can't get around much 'cause my feet and legs bother me, but I got good eyes an' good ears an' all my own teeth. I ain't never had a bad tooth in my head. Yes'm, I'm eighty-one, going on eighty-two. Marster done wrote my age down in his book where he kept the names of all his colored folks. Muh [Mother] belonged to Dr. Jones, but Pappy belonged to Marse Israel Lash over yonder [points northwest]. Younguns always went with their mammies, so I belonged to the Joneses. Muh and Pappy could visit back and forth sometimes, but they never lived together till after freedom. Yes'm, we was happy. We got plenty to eat. Marster and old Miss Julia [Dr. Jones's wife, matriarch of the whole plantation] was mighty strict, but they was good to us. Colored folks on some of the other plantations wasn't so lucky. Some of 'em had overseers, mean, cruel men. On one plantation, the field hands had to hustle to get to the end of the row at eleven o'clock dinner time, 'cause when the cooks brought their dinner they had to stop just where they was and eat, an' the sun was mighty hot out in those fields. They only had ashcakes [corn pone baked in ashes] without salt and molasses for their dinner, but we had beans an' grits an' salt an' sometimes meat.

"I was lucky. Miss Ella [daughter of the first Beverly Jones] was a little girl when I was borned, and she claimed me. We played together an' grew up together. I waited on her an' most times slept on the floor in her room. Muh was cook, an' when I done got big enough I helped to set the table in the big dinin' room. Then I'd put on a clean white apron an' carry in the vict-uals an' stand behind Miss Ella's chair. She'd fix me a piece of somethin' from her plate an' hand it back over her shoulder to me [eloquent hands illustrate Miss Ella's making of a sandwich]. I'd take it an' run outside to eat it. Then I'd wipe my mouth an' go back to stand behind Miss Ella again an' maybe get another snack.

"Yes'm, there was a crowd of hands on the plantation. I 'mind [remember] 'em all, an' I can 'call most of their names. Mac, Curley, William, Sanford, Lewis, Henry, Ed, Sylvester, Hamp, an' Juke was the menfolks. The women was Hellie, two Lucys, Martha, Nervie, Jane, Laura, Fannie, Lizzie, Cassie, Tensie, Lindy, an' Mary Jane. The women mostly worked in the house. There was always two washwomen, a cook, some hands to help her, two sewin' women, a house girl, an' some who did all the weavin' an' spinnin'. The men worked in the fields an' yard. One was stable boss an' looked after all the horses an' mules. We raised our own flax an' cotton an' wool, spun the thread, wove the cloth, made all the clothes. Yes'm, we made the men's shirts an' pants an' coats. One woman knitted all the stockings for the white folks an' colored folks, too. I 'mind she had one finger all twisted an' stiff from holdin' her knittin' needles. We wove the cotton an' linen for sheets an' pillow slips an' table covers. We wove the wool blankets, too. I use to wait on the girl who did the weavin'. When she took the cloth off the loom, she done give me the thrums [ends of thread left on the loom]. I tied 'em all together with teensy little knots an' got me some scraps from the sewin' room, and I made me some quilt tops. Some of 'em was real pretty, too! [Pride of workmanship is evidenced by a toss of Betty's head.]

"All our spinnin' wheels and flax wheels and looms was handmade by a wheelwright, Marse Noah Westmoreland. He lived over yonder [a thumb indicates north]. Those old wheels are still in the family. I got one of the flax wheels. Miss Ella done give it to me for a present. Leather was tanned an' shoes was made on the place. Course, the hands mostly went barefoot in warm weather, white chillun, too. We had our own mill to grind the wheat and corn, an' we raised all our meat. We made our own candles from tallow and beeswax. I 'spect some of the old candle molds are over to the house now. We wove our own candlewicks, too. I never saw a match till I was a grown woman. We made our fire with flint an' punk [rotten wood]. Yes'm, I was trained to cook an' clean an' sew. I learned to make men's pants an' coats. First coat I made, Miss Julia told me to rip the collar off, an' by the time I picked out all the teensy stitches an' sewed it together again I could set a collar right. I can do it today, too! [Again there is manifested a good workman's pardonable pride of achievement.]

"Miss Julia cut out all the clothes herself for men and women, too. I 'spect her big shears an' patterns an' old cuttin' table are over at the house now. Miss Julia cut out all the clothes, an' then the colored girls sewed 'em up, but she looked 'em all over, and they better be sewed right! Miss Julia bossed the whole plantation. She looked after the sick folks and sent the doctor [Dr. Jones] to dose 'em, and she carried the keys to the store-rooms and pantries.

"Yes'm, I'm some educated. Muh showed me my ABCs and my numbers, and when I was fifteen I went to school in the log church built by the Moravians. They give it to the colored folks to use for their own school and church. [This log house is still standing near Bethania.] Our teacher was a white man, Marse Fulk. He had one eye, done lost the other in the war. We didn't have no colored teachers then. They wasn't educated. We 'tended school four months a year. I went through the fifth reader, the

North Carolina reader. I can figure a little an' read some, but I can't write much 'cause my fingers are all stiffened up. Miss Julia use to read the Bible to us an' tell us right an' wrong, and Muh showed me all she could, an' so did the other colored folks. Mostly, they was kind to each other.

"No'm, I don't know much about spells an' charms. Course, most of the old folks believed in 'em. One colored man use to make charms, little bags filled with queer things. He called 'em 'jacks' an' sold 'em to the colored folks an' some white folks, too.

"Yes'm, I saw some slaves sold away from the plantation— four men and two women, both of 'em with little babies. The traders got 'em. Sold 'em down to Mobile, Alabama. One was my pappy's sister. We never heard from her again. I saw a likely young feller sold for fifteen hundred dollars. That was my uncle Ike. Marse Jonathan Spease bought him and kept him the rest of his life.

"Yes'm, we saw Yankee soldiers [Stoneman's Cavalry in 1865]. They come marchin' by and stopped at the house. I wasn't scared 'cause they was all talkin' and laughin' and friendly, but they sure was hungry. They dumped the wet clothes out of the big wash pot in the yard and filled it with water. Then they broke into the smokehouse and got a lot of hams and boiled 'em in the pot and ate 'em right there in the yard. The women cooked up a lot of corn pone for 'em, and coffee, too. Marster had a barrel of liquor put by, an' the Yankees knocked the head in an' filled their canteens. There wasn't nary drop left. When we heard the soldiers comin', our boys turned the horses loose in the woods. The Yankees said they had to have 'em an' would burn the house down if we didn't get 'em. So our boys whistled up the horses, an' the soldiers carried 'em all off. They carried off ol' Jennie mule, too, but let little Jack mule go. When the soldiers was gone, the stable boss said, 'If ol' Jennie mule once gets loose, nobody on earth can catch her unless she wants. She'll be back!' Sure enough, in a couple of days, she come home by herself, an' we worked the farm just with her an' little Jack.

"Some of the colored folks followed the Yankees away. Five or six of our boys went. Two of 'em traveled as far as Yadkinville but come back. The rest of 'em kept goin', an' we never heard tell of 'em again.

"Yes'm, when we was freed, Pappy come to get Muh and me. We stayed around here. Where could we go? These was our folks, and I couldn't go far away from Miss Ella. We moved out near Rural Hall [some five miles from Bethania], an' Pappy farmed, but I worked at the homeplace a lot.

"When I was about twenty-four, Marse R. J. Reynolds come from Virginia an' set up a tobacco factory. He fetched some hands with him. One was a likely young feller named Cofer, from Patrick County, Virginia. I liked him, an' we got married an' moved back here to my folks [the Jones family]. We started to buy our little place an' raise a family. I done had four chillun, but two's dead. I got grandchillun and great-grandchillun close by. This is home to us. When we talk about the old homeplace [the Jones residence, now some hundred years old], we just say 'the house' 'cause there's only one house to us. The rest of the family was all fine folks and good to me, but I loved Miss Ella better'n anyone or anythin' else in the world. She was the best friend I ever had. If I ever wanted for anythin', I just asked her, an' she give it to me or got it for me somehow. Once when Cofer was in his last sickness, his sister come from East Liverpool, Ohio, to see him. I went to Miss Ella to borrow a little money. She didn't have no change, but she just took a ten-dollar bill from her purse an' says, 'Here you are, Betty, use what you need and bring me what's left.'

"I always did what I could for her, too, an' stood by her—but one time. That was when we was little girls goin' together to fetch the mail. It was hot an' dusty, an' we stopped to cool off an' wade in the branch. We heard a horse trottin' an' looked up, an' there was Marster switchin' his ridin' whip an' lookin' at us. 'Get for home, you two, and I'll tend to you,' he says, an' we got! But this time, I let Miss Ella go to the house alone, an' I sneaked around to Granny's cabin an' hid. I was afraid I'd get whupped! 'Nother time, Miss Ella went to town an' told me to keep up her fire whilst she was away. I fell asleep on the hearth and the fire done burnt out, so's when Miss Ella come home the room was cold. She was mad as hops. Said she never had hit me, but she sure felt like doin' it then.

"Yes'm, I been here a right smart while. I done lived to see three generations of my white folks come an' go, an' they're the finest folks on earth. There use to be a regular buryin' ground for the plantation hands. The colored chillun use to play there, but I always played with the white chillun. [This accounts for Aunt Betty's gentle manner and speech.] Three of the old log cabins [slave cabins] is there yet. One of 'em was the boys' cabin [a house for boys and unmarried men]. They've got walls a foot thick an' are used for storerooms now. After freedom, we buried out around our little churches, but some of the old grounds are plowed under an' turned into pasture 'cause the colored folks didn't get no deeds to 'em. It won't be long 'fore I go, too, but I'm gwine lie near my old home an' my folks.

"Yes'm, I remember Marse Israel Lash, my pappy's marster. He was a low, thick-set man, very jolly an' friendly. He was real smart an' good, too, 'cause his colored folks all loved him. He worked in the bank, an' when the Yankees come, 'stead of shuttin' the door 'gainst 'em like the others did, he bid 'em welcome. [Betty's nodding head, expansive smile, and widespread hands eloquently pantomime the banker's greeting.] So the Yankees done took the bank but give it back to him for his very own, an' he kept it, but there was lots of bad feelin' 'cause he never give folks the money they put in the old bank. [Possibly, this explains the closing of the branch of the Cape Fear Bank in Salem and the opening of Israel Lash's own institution, the First National Bank of Salem, in 1866.]

"I saw General Robert E. Lee, too. After the war, he come with some friends to a meeting at Five Forks Baptist Church. All the white folks gathered round an' shook his hand, an' I peeked 'tween their legs an' got a good look at him. But he didn't have no whiskers, he was smooth-face! [Pictures of General Lee all show him with beard and mustache.]

"Miss Ella died two years ago. I was sick in the hospital, but the doctor come to tell me. I couldn't go to her buryin'. I sure missed her. [Poignant grief moistens Betty's eyes and thickens her voice.] There wasn't ever no one like her. Miss Kate an' young Miss Julia still live at the house with their brother, Marse Lucian [all children of the first Beverly Jones and old Miss Julia], but it don't seem right with Miss Ella gone. Life seems different somehow, though there lots of my young white folks an' my own kin livin' round, an' they're real good to me. But Miss Ella's gone!

"Good day, ma'am. Come anytime. You're welcome to. I'm right glad to have visitors 'cause I can't get out much." [A bobbing little curtsy accompanies Betty's cordial farewell.]

BETTY QUESNESBERRY

Born: 1859
Age: Seventy-seven
Master: None
Place: Crawford County, Arkansas
Interviewer: Ollie Frasier
Source: Second Supplemental Series, Arkansas Narratives,
    volume 01T, page 117

On entering the home of a very refined, dignified old lady of Van Buren, Arkansas, one is impressed with the age of the well-preserved surroundings. Over the fireplace hangs an oil painting three feet square which is more than one hundred years old. This is the picture of her grandfather, who was a big slaveholder in Virginia. Some of the slaves born on his plantation were sent to his son at Van Buren, and the early life of this estimable lady was greatly influenced by them. Some of her earliest memories are the Negro theology she learned from her black "mammy."

According to her "mammy," the devil kept a tub of some molten mass placed on rocks over a fire and threw all bad children into it. The devil, a hideous-looking character with horns, hoofs, and a tail, stood near the tub with a pitchfork in his hand, and if one of the children attempted to escape he threw it back into the tub with the pitchfork. The child's fears were allayed by telling her that children under seven years old were not held responsible for their wrongdoings, but that their parents were responsible for their conduct until they reached their seventh birthdays.

The child was very much disturbed and carried this information to her mother. The mother assured her that this was only one of "Mammy's" sayings, but the little daughter came back with the inquiry as to whether the parents were accountable for the behavior of small children. When the mother answered in the affirmative, the matter was dismissed from the young mind.

"Mammy" also told the youngster of her undoubted experience with witches. The Negro said that a woman who lived near her was bewitching her. Each night after she had retired and gone to sleep, the witch would jump on her and ride her all night. This continued for a year, and the Negro, growing thin and weak, was acquiring the resemblance of the witch. Finally, a friend gave her the following remedy, which released her from the witch's power. Molasses, vinegar, water, and rusty nails were put into a jug and portions of it taken daily. The Negro was freed and soon regained her strength.

The bond between this child, Betty Greene, who is now Mrs. Quesnesberry, and her Negro "mammy" was very close. After the death of Betty's parents and the dissolution of the Greene home, "Mammy" was hired by another family to cook. When Betty married, the lady for whom "Mammy" was working said, "I'll lose my cook." Mrs. Quesnesberry told her that she would not think of such a thing as taking her servant from her, but the other lady replied that when she hired "Mammy" she told her that she would stay with her until "Miss Betty" married, and then she would go with her.

"Mammy's" loyalty was put to a test at another time when a gentleman from St. Louis was visiting in the Quesnesberry home. Complimentary to her cooking, the gentleman told Mrs. Quesnesberry that he would like to have her cook. Mrs. Quesnesberry was sure that "Mammy" wouldn't leave her, but to show the Negro's loyalty called, "Mammy, come here. This gentleman wants to hire you and take you to St. Louis to work in his home. He can pay you much more than I, and it would be a good place for you." "Mammy" stood with her head down for a minute and then said, "I don't want to leave you, Miss Betty, to go anywhere." She died in the Quesnesberry home.

Referring to Negro spirituals, Mrs. Quesnesberry said they were close to her heart. A short time ago, this aged lady was in the dusky room alone as the twilight was changing into night. She turned on the radio and some voice was singing "I'm Going Home." Her first thought was "That's Mammy's song," and then she wondered if "Mammy" was singing that song in the great beyond, and she couldn't keep back the tears. When she related the incident, her glasses had to be removed and her eyes rubbed.

Mrs. Quesnesberry remembers another incident connected with her father, Judge Greene, who was a very prominent lawyer in the early days of Van Buren, and his loyal slaves. Mrs. Quesnesberry said that she was a small child and had very little conception of numbers, but that it seemed to her that her father owned as many as one hundred slaves, and she was positive there were as many as fifty. During the Civil War, word came that the Federal army was moving into the town. Judge Greene decided to take his slaves to Texas, and they, with the stock, were set across the Arkansas River late one afternoon, where they were to await his coming the following morning. Judge Greene had never been accustomed to driving, but since the Negro horsemen were away it was necessary for him to do his own driving. Taking a sixteen-year-old Negro girl who was unable to go with the slaves on the previous afternoon, he got into his buggy and started on the long journey. As he was going up the hill in Van Buren, the horses became frightened, and due to his inefficiency as a driver the buggy was overturned and he was badly injured. He was returned to his home suffering from a head injury and a badly mangled arm, which had to be amputated. He passed away six weeks later. When the slaves learned of the accident, they returned home to their masters instead of trying to secure their freedom. As was expected, Blount's army moved into town. Every home in Van Buren except that of Judge Greene was raided. Loyal to their master, the slaves patrolled the grounds and forbade the soldiers entering, telling them that the judge was very sick. The men questioned their story, but the slaves were so positive that the troops did not molest them.

Finally, a hospital flag was placed in front of the residence. Before the judge's death, he requested the fifteen slaves who had done the work in the home to stay with his wife. Again, their loyalty was shown in their complying to his wishes. After the Emancipation Proclamation, the slaves who labored in the fields went their ways, but the fifteen house servants remained with Mrs. Greene and her family.

Friends and Families

"If ve see a person loaded vid bundles and he is old and barely able to go, ve gif a hand. See, ve Jews, you colored, but ve know no difference. Anyone needing help, ve gif."

Julia Brown interview

Tempie Herndon Durham, ca. 1936-1938
Library of Congress, Manuscript Division
(interview on pages 52-57)

Friends and Families

The center of the enslaved community was the family; it was the primary means of survival. However, the definition and nature of what constituted that family make for one of the most critical and enduring discussions of the institution of slavery. Within the ex-slave narratives, the definition of family remains pretty liberal, even extending unto—as uncomfortable as is this declaration—the slave owners themselves. Beyond the immediate and extended family, the network of relations in the enslaved community included other kin, coworkers, neighbors, merchants, church members, professionals, and even supporters in the community opposed to slavery.

Marriage was a complicated institution within the landscape of the Southern agricultural homestead. Slave husbands often lived in different households, thereby forcing the women to assume greater independence and autonomy within the social and cultural institutions of the slave community. Whereas traditional backgrounds in Africa supported an interconnected network, the commerce in human commodities often shredded families of their partners, their children, their kin, and even their very existence as a "family." Husbands and wives played complementary, egalitarian roles to a degree often misunderstood both by contemporary and subsequent historians.

When mothers were quickly forced to return to the "big house" and the fields to assume their tasks, grandmothers and siblings took on many of the responsibilities of child rearing. Since the responsibilities of enslaved women included both their own families and the slave owners' families, the lines of distinction between the two became blurred. This often brought enslaved women into conflict with their "mistresses," but at other times built tenuous bonds of solidarity between "sisters" who shared the same gender yet lived across an unfathomable racial divide.

The focus of the enslaved woman's life was on the material production for and support of the slaveholder's family. As such, she lived and worked in a community of her peers that was largely female. Bonds of friendship and interdependence were formed that transcended the task system and provided a network of support. According to Deborah Gray White, "many bonded females could forge their own independent definition of womanhood through the female network, a definition to which they could relate on the basis of their own notions about what women should be and how they should act."[24]

The following section of narratives offers a glimpse of the slave community. The first interviewee, Rosa Starke of Winnsboro, South Carolina, belonged to one of the most prominent and historic families of the South Carolina Upcountry. Colonel Nicholas Peay, her owner, was one of the richest men in Fairfield County and a veteran of the Seminole Wars whose vast estates spread across many plantations and who owned so many slaves they could hardly be counted. Rosa's story reveals not only the class divisions of "white folks" but how class and gender played out within the slave community in the social distinctions between the "house nigger" and the "common field-hand nigger." As Rosa puts it, crossing the lines of social class in courtship "offend de white folks, specially de young misses, who liked de business of matchmakin' and matin' of de young slaves."

The next narrative is that of Tempie Herndon Durham from the Piedmont area of North Carolina, who was reportedly 103 years old at the time of her interview and whose master raised sheep and ran a spinning room. What is most interesting about Tempie's story is the slice-of-life portrait it gives of the social life of her community and an owner who cared enough about the people in his midst to make their lives less harsh. The Herndons put on a fancy wedding for Tempie and her husband, even to the point of making a big wedding cake "wid a bride an' groom standin' in de middle holdin' hands." Indeed, the mistress "played de weddin' march on de piano." Should readers lapse into a sense of comfort about her environment, she reminds them of the indisputable fact of her enslavement: "After de weddin', we went down to de cabin Miss Betsy done all dressed up, but Exeter couldn't stay no longer dan dat night 'cause he belonged to Marse Snipes Durham, an' he had to go back home."

For Lula Jackson, the subject of the next narrative, tragedy and accidental death are like a member of the family. As her family included nearly twenty siblings, it is understandable how she could tolerate the misfortune. Her father's mother was enslaved by a master named Hurt who "had an awful name, and he was an awful man." He would whip the slaves until they blistered, then cut open the blisters and drop sealing wax into them. Lula's grandmother was taken from him when she was struck by lightning and killed. Her mother's first husband was killed after he challenged a younger man to a wrestling match and was thrown to his death; her mother's second husband was a preacher who died after catching pneumonia walking in the rain to visit his daughter. Lula's brother-in-law was killed by a horse. Her own husband was dragged to death by a mule. As he lay dying, he said to his friend, "See this little woman of mine? I hate to leave her. She's just such a good little woman. She ain't got no business in this world without a husband." She never remarried.

The next two narratives, both from Georgia, are a fascinating study in the dynamics of race and gender in Southern society and how they played out in the ex-slave narratives. The interviewers have prominent roles in both narratives, almost to the extent of becoming characters; both presentations are shaped by the interviewers in a creative manner that undermines their credibility as objective sources of information. The first interview is conducted by Geneva Tonsill, one of the few black interviewers hired by the Federal Writers' Project, a married mother of three whose husband was a public-school teacher in Atlanta.[25] The second is conducted by Sarah H. Hall, a widow and former librarian at the University of Georgia whose aunt had grown up with the interviewee on Sarah's grandfather's plantation.[26] Reading the two parallel narratives provides insight into more than just the lives of the interviewees; seldom in the WPA ex-slave narratives is there such a study in contradictions.

The last narrative is yet another curiosity. From Warren County, Mississippi, and a section entitled "Mississippi Folklore" comes an entry called "Slavery Cooking" that is basically a collection of recipes from the slave community. The women cooks, who show up in no other place in the ex-slave narratives, offer recipes for ashcakes, roast suckling pig, fried chicken, greens and dumplings, persimmon loaf, squirrel pie, and potato pone. One of the delicacies described is fire-baked raccoon; Ellen Gooden considers herself "de best coon cooker dere is." "You didn't ever hear of cooking make nobody sick in dem days, lessen dey ate too much," says ex-slave Marry Joiner.

ROSA STARKE

Born: 1854
Age: Eighty-three
Master: Colonel Nicholas Peay
Place: Fairfield County, South Carolina
Interviewer: W. W. Dixon
Source: First Series, Library of Congress Rare Book Room
Collection, South Carolina Narratives, volume 03B,
page 147

*Rosa's grandfather was a slave of Solicitor Starke.
Although she has had two husbands since slavery, she has
thrown their names into the discard and goes by the name
of Rosa Starke. She lives in a three-room frame house with
her son, John Harrison, two miles south of Winnsboro, South
Carolina, on the plantation of Mrs. Rebecca V. Woodward.
She still does farm work, hoeing and picking cotton.*

"They say I was six years old when de war commence
poppin' in Charleston. Mammy and Pappy say dat I was born
on de Graham place, one of de nineteen plantations of my old
marster, Nick Peay, in 1854. My pappy was name Bob, and my

mammy name Salina. They had belonged to old Marse Tom Starke befo' old Marse Nick bought them. My brudders was name Bob and John. I had a sister name Carrie. They was all older than me.

"My marster, Nick Peay, had nineteen places, wid a overseer and slave quarters on every place. Folks dat knows will tell you, dis day, dat them nineteen plantations, in all, was twenty-seven thousand acres. He had a thousand slaves, more or less, too many to take a census of. Befo' de numerator get round, some more would be born or bought, and de numerator had to be sent round by Marse Nick, so old Miss Martha, our mistress, say. Her never could know just how many 'twas. Folks used to come to see her and ask how many they had, and her say it was one of them sums in de 'rithmetic dat a body never could take a slate and pencil and find out de correct answer to.

"Her was a Adamson befo' her marry old Marster, a grand big buckra. Had a grand manner, no patience wid poor white folks. They couldn't come in de front yard; they knowed to pass on by to de lot, hitch up dere hoss, and come knock on de kitchen door and make dere wants and wishes knowed to de butler.

"You wants me to tell 'bout what kind of house us niggers live in then? Well, it 'pend on de nigger and what him was doin'. Dere was just two classes to de white folks—buckra slave owners and poor white folks dat didn't own no slaves. Dere was more classes 'mongst de slaves. De first class was de house servants. Dese was de butler, de maids, de nurses, chambermaids, and de cooks. De next class was de carriage drivers and de gardeners, de carpenters, de barber, and de stablemen. Then come de next class—de wheelwright, wagoners, blacksmiths, and slave foremen. De next class I 'members was de cow men and de niggers dat have care of de dogs. All dese have good houses and never have to work hard or get a beatin'. Then come de cradlers of de wheat, de threshers, and de millers of de corn and de wheat, and de feeders of de cotton gin. De lowest class was de common field niggers. A house nigger man might swoop down and mate wid a field hand's good-lookin' daughter now and then, for pure love of her, but you never see a house gal lower herself by marryin' and matin' wid a common field-hand nigger. Dat offend de white folks, specially de young misses, who liked de business of matchmakin' and matin' of de young slaves.

"My young marsters was Marse Tom, Marse Nick, and Marse Austin. My young misses was Miss Martha, Miss Mary, and Miss Anne Eliza. I knows Marse Nick Jr. marry a Cunningham of Liberty Hill. Marse Tom marry a Lyles, and Marse Austin marry and move to Abbeville after de war. Old Marster die de year befo' de war, I think, 'cause my mammy and pappy fell in de division to Marse Nick, and us leave de Graham place to go to de homeplace. It was called de Melrose Place. And what a place dat was! 'Twas on a hill overlookin' de place where de Longtown Presbyterian Church and cemetery is today. Dere was thirty rooms in it and a fish pond on top of it. A flower yard stretched clean down de hill to de big road, where de big gate, hangin' on big granite pillars, swung open to let de carriages, buggies, and wagons in and up to de house.

"Can I tell you some of de things dat was in dat house when de Yankees come? Golly not! Dat I can't, but I 'members some things dat would 'stonish you as it 'stonished them. They had Marseille carpets, linen tablecloths, two silver candlesticks in every room, four wine decanters, four nutcrackers, and two coffeepots, all of them silver. Silver casters for pepper, salt, and vinegar bottles. All de plates was china. Ninety-eight silver folks, knives, teaspoons, and tablespoons. Four silver ladles, six silver sugar tongs, silver goblets, a silver mustard pot, and two silver fruit stands. All de fireplaces had brass firedogs [andirons] and marble mantelpieces. Dere was four oil paintings in de hall; each cost, so Marse Nick say, one hundred dollars. One was his ma, one was his pa, one was his uncle Austin, and de other was of Colonel Lamar.

"De smokehouse had four rooms and a cellar. One room, every year, was filled wid brown sugar just shoveled in wid spades. In winter, they would drive up a drove of hogs from each plantation, kill them, scald de hair off them, and pack de meat away in salt, and hang up de hams and shoulders round and 'bout de smokehouse. Most of de rum and wine was kept in barrels in de cellar, but dere was a closet in de house where whiskey and brandy was kept for quick use. All back on de east side of de mansion was de garden and terraces, acres of sweet taters, water millions [watermelons] and strawberries and two long rows of beehives.

"Old Marster die. De 'praisers of de 'state come and figure dat his mules, niggers, cows, hogs, and things was worth $200,000. Land and houses I disremember 'bout. They, anyhow, say de property was over $1 million. They put a price of $1,600 on Mammy and $1,800 on Pappy. I 'member they say I was worth $400. Young Marse Nick tell us dat the personal property of de estate was 'praised at $288,168.78.

"De Yankees come set all de cotton and de gin house afire. Load up all de meat, take some of de sugar and shovel some over de yard, take all de wine, rum, and liquor, gut de house of all de silver and valuables, set it afire, and leave one thousand niggers cold and hungry, and our white folks in a misery they never has got over to de third generation of them. Some of them is de poorest white folks in dis state today. I weeps when I sees them so poor, but they is 'spectable yet, thank God.

"After de war, I stuck to de Peay white folks till I got married to Will Harrison. I can't say I love him, though he was de father of all my chillun. My pappy, you know, was a half-white man.

Maybe dat explain it. Anyhow, when he took de fever, I sent for Dr. Gibson, who tend him faithful, but he die. I felt more like I was free when I come back from de funeral than I did when Marse Abe Lincoln set us free.

"I next marry, in a halfhearted way, John Pearson, to help take care of me and my three chillun, John, Bob, and Carrie. Him take pneumonia and die, and I never have a speck of heart to marry a colored man since. I just have a mind to wait for de proper sort till I get to heaven, but dese adult teachers destroy dat hope. They read me dat dere is no marryin' in heaven. Well, well, dat'll be a great disappointment to some I knows, both white and black, and de ginger-cake women like me.

"Is I got any more to tell you? Just dis: Dere was 365 windows and doors to Marse Nick Peay's house at Melrose, one for every day in de year, my mistress 'low. And dere was a peach tree in de orchard so grafted dat peach tree have ripe peaches on it in May, June, July, August, September, and October."

TEMPIE HERNDON DURHAM

Born: 1834
Age: 103
Master: George Herndon
Place: Chatham County, North Carolina
Interviewer: Travis Jordan
Source: First Series, Library of Congress Rare Book Room
Collection, North Carolina Narratives, volume 14A,
page 284

"I was thirty-one years ol' when de surrender come. Dat makes me sho nuff ol'. Near 'bout a hundred an' three years done passed over dis here white head of mine. I's been here, I mean I's been here. 'Spects I's de oldest nigger in Durham. I's been here so long dat I done forgot near 'bout as much as dese here new-generation niggers knows or ever gwine know.

"My white folks lived in Chatham County. Dey was Marse George an' Miss Betsy Herndon. Miss Betsy was a Snipes befo' she married Marse George. Dey had a big plantation an' raised corn, wheat, cotton, an' tobacco. I don't know how many field niggers Marse George had, but he had a mess of 'em, an' he had hosses, too, an' cows, hogs, an' sheeps. He raised sheeps an' sold de wool, an' dey used de wool at de big house, too. Dey was a big weavin' room where de blankets was wove, an' dey wove de cloth for de winter clothes, too. Linda Herndon an' Milla Edwards was de head weavers. Dey looked after de weavin' of de fancy blankets. Miss Betsy was a good weaver, too. She weave de same as de niggers. She say she love de clackin' sound of de loom an' de way de shuttles run in an' out carryin' a long tail of bright-colored thread. Some days, she set at de loom all de mornin' peddlin' wid her feets an' her white hands flittin' over de bobbins.

"De cardin' an' spinnin' room was full of niggers. I can hear dem spinnin' wheels now turnin' round an' sayin' *hum-m-m-m, hum-m-m-m*, an' hear de slaves singin' while dey spin. Mammy Rachel stayed in de dyein' room. Dey wasn't nothin' she didn't know 'bout dyein'. She knew every kind of root, bark, leaf, an' berry dat made red, blue, green, or whatever color she wanted. Dey had a big shelter where de dye pots set over de coals. Mammy Rachel would fill de pots wid water, then she put in de roots, bark, an' stuff an' boil de juice out, then she strain it an' put in de salt an' vinegar to set de color. After de wool an' cotton done been carded an' spun to thread, Mammy take de hanks an' drop 'em in de pot of boilin' dye. She stir 'em round an' lift 'em up an' down wid a stick, an' when she hang 'em up on de line in de sun, dey was every color of de rainbow. When dey dripped dry, dey was sent to de weavin' room, where dey was wove in blankets an' things.

"When I growed up, I married Exeter Durham. He belonged to Marse Snipes Durham, who had de plantation 'cross de county line in Orange County. We had a big weddin'. We was married on de front porch of de big house. Marse George killed a shoat, an' Miss Betsy had Georgianna, de cook, to bake a big weddin' cake all iced up white as snow wid a bride an' groom standin' in de middle holdin' hands. De table was set out in de yard under de trees, an' you ain't never seed de like of eats. All de niggers come to de feast, an' Marse George had a dram for everybody. Dat was some weddin'. I had on a white dress, white shoes, an' long white gloves dat come to my elbow, an' Miss Betsy done made me a weddin' veil out of a white net window curtain. When she played de weddin' march on de piano, me an' Exeter marched down de walk an' up on de porch to de altar Miss Betsy done fixed. Dat de prettiest altar I ever seed. Back 'gainst de rose vine dat was full of red roses, Miss Betsy done put tables filled wid flowers an' white candles. She done spread down a bedsheet, a sho-nuff linen sheet, for us to stand on, an' dey was a white pillow to kneel down on. Exeter done made me a weddin' ring. He made it out of a big red button wid his pocketknife. He done cut it so round an' polished it so smooth dat it looked like a red satin ribbon tied round my finger. Dat sho was a pretty ring. I wore it 'bout fifty years, den it got so thin dat I lost it one day in de washtub when I was washin' clothes.

"Uncle Edmond Kirby married us. He was de nigger preacher dat preached at de plantation church. After Uncle Edmond said de last words over me an' Exeter, Marse George got to have his little fun. He say, 'Come on, Exeter, you an' Tempie got to jump over de broomstick backwards. You got to do dat to see which one gwine be boss of your household.' Everybody come stand round to watch. Marse George hold de broom 'bout a foot high off de floor. De one dat jump over it backwards an' never touch de handle gwine boss de house, an' if both of 'em jump over without touchin' it, dey won't gwine be no bossin', dey just gwine be genial. I jumped first, an' you ought to seed me. I sailed right over dat broomstick same as a cricket, but when Exeter jump he done had a big dram an' his feets was so big an' clumsy dat dey got all tangled up in dat broom, an' he fell headlong. Marse George, he laugh an' laugh, an' told Exeter he gwine be bossed till he scared to speak lessen I told him to speak.

"After de weddin', we went down to de cabin Miss Betsy done all dressed up, but Exeter couldn't stay no longer dan dat night 'cause he belonged to Marse Snipes Durham, an' he had to go back home. He left de next day for his plantation, but he come back every Saturday night an' stay till Sunday night. We had eleven chillun. Nine was born befo' surrender an' two after we was set free. So I had two chillun dat wasn't born in bondage. I was worth a heap to Marse George 'cause I had so many chillun. De more chillun a slave had, de more dey was worth. Lucy Carter was de only nigger on de plantation dat had more chillun dan I had. She had twelve, but her chillun was sickly an' mine was muley strong an' healthy. Dey never was sick.

"When de war come, Marse George was too ol' to go, but young Marse Bill went. He went an' took my brother Sim wid him. Marse Bill took Sim along to look after his hoss an' everything. Dey didn't neither one get shot, but Miss Betsy was scared near 'bout to death all de time, scared dey was gwine be brung home shot all to pieces like some of de soldiers was.

"De Yankees wasn't so bad. De most dey wanted was somethin' to eat. Dey was all de time hungry. De first thing dey ask for when dey come was somethin' to put in dey stomach. An' chicken! I ain't never seed even a preacher eat chicken like dem Yankees. I believes to my soul dey ain't never seed no chicken till dey come down here. An' hot biscuit, too. I seed a passel of 'em eat up a whole sack of flour one night for supper. Georgianna sift flour till she look white an' dusty as a miller. Dem soldiers didn't turn down no ham neither. Dat de onliest thing dey took from Marse George. Dey went in de smokehouse an' toted off de hams an' shoulders. Marse George say he come off mighty light if dat all dey want, 'sides he got plenty of shoats anyhow.

"We had all de eats we wanted while de war was shootin' dem guns 'cause Marse George was home an' he kept de niggers workin'. We had chickens, gooses, meat, peas, flour, meal, potatoes, an' things like dat all de time, an' milk an' butter, too, but we didn't have no sugar an' coffee. We used ground parched corn for coffee an' cane 'lasses [sugarcane molasses] for sweetenin'. Dat wasn't so bad wid a heap of thick cream. Anyhow, we had enough to eat to provide wid de neighbors dat didn't have none when surrender come.

"I was glad when de war stopped 'cause den me an' Exeter could be together all de time, 'stead of Saturday an' Sunday. After we was free, we lived right on at Marse George's plantation a long time. We rented de land for a fourth of what we made, den after a while we bought a farm. We paid three hundred dollars we done saved. We had a hoss, a steer, a cow, an' two pigs, 'sides some chickens an' four geese. Miss Betsy went up in de attic an' give us a bed an' bed tick. She give us enough goose feathers to make two pillows, den she give us a table an' some chairs. She give us some dishes, too. Marse George give Exeter a bushel of seed corn an' some seed wheat, den he told him to go down to de barn an' get a bag of cottonseed. We got all dis, den we hitched up de wagon an' throwed in de passel of chillun an' moved to our new farm, an' de chillun was put to work in de field. Dey growed up in de field 'cause dey was put to work time dey could walk good.

"Freedom is all right, but de niggers was better off befo' surrender, 'cause den dey was looked after an' dey didn't get in no trouble fightin' an' killin' like dey do dese days. If a nigger cut up an' got sassy in slavery times, his ol' marse give him a good whippin', an' he went back an' set down an' behaved hisself. If he was sick, Marse an' Missus looked after him, an' if he needed store medicine it was bought an' give to him; he didn't have to pay nothin'. Dey didn't even have to think 'bout clothes nor nothin' like dat; dey was made an' give to 'em. Maybe everybody's marse an' missus wasn't good as Marse George an' Miss Betsy, but dey was de same as a mammy an' pappy to us niggers."

LULA JACKSON

Born: 1858
Age: Seventy-nine
Master: Early Hurt
Place: Russell County, Alabama
Interviewer: Samuel Taylor
Source: First Series, Library of Congress Rare Book Room
    Collection, Arkansas Narratives, volume 09B, page 9

"I was born in Alabama, Russell County, on a place called Sand Ridge, about seven miles out from Columbus, Georgia. Bred and born in Alabama. Come out here a young gal. Wasn't married when I come out here. Married when a boy from Alabama met me, though. Got his picture. Lula Williams! That was my name before I married. 'How many sisters do you have?' That's another question they ask all the time; I suppose you want to know, too. Two. 'Where are they?' That's another one of them questions they always askin' me. You want to know it, too? I got one in Clarksdale, Mississippi. And the other one is in Philadelphia. No, I mean in Philipp city, Tallahatchie [County]. Her name is Bertha Owens, and she lives in Philipp city. 'What state is Philipp city in?' That'll be the next question. It is in Mississippi, sir. Now, is there anything else you'd like to know?

"My mother's name was Bertha Williams, and my father's name was Fred Williams. I don't know nothing 'bout Mama's mother. Yes, her name was Crecie. My father's mother was named Sarah. She got killed by lightning. Crecie's husband was named John Oliver. Sarah's husband was named William Daniel. Early Hurt was Mama's master. He had an awful name, and he was an awful man. He whipped you till he'd bloodied you and blistered you. Then he would cut open the blisters and drop sealing wax in them and in the open wounds made by the whips.

"When the Yankees come in, his wife run in and got in the bed between the mattresses. I don't see why it didn't kill her. I don't know how she stood it. Early died when the Yankees come in. He was already sick. The Yankees come in and said, 'Did you know you are on the Yankee line?' He said, 'No, by God, when did that happen?' They said, 'It happened tonight, G-- d--- you.' And he turned right on over and done everything on hisself and died. He had a eatin' cancer on his shoulder.

"My mother had so many children that I didn't get to go to school much. She had nineteen children, and I had to stay home and work to help take care of them. I can't write at all.

"I went to school in Alabama, round on a colored man's place—Mr. Winters. That was near a little town called Fort Mitchell and Silver Rim, where they put the men in jail. I was a child. Mrs. Smith, a white woman from the North, was the second teacher that I had. The first was Mr. Croler. My third teacher was a man named Mr. Nelson. All of these was white. They wasn't colored teachers. After the war, that was. I have the book I used when I went to school. Here is the little arithmetic [book] I used. Here is the Blue Back Speller. I have a McGuffy's Primer, too. I didn't use that. I got that out of the trash basket at the white people's house where I work. One day, they throwed it out. That is what they use now, ain't it?

"Here is a book my husband give me. He bought it for me because I told him I wanted a Second Reader. He said, 'Well, I'll go up to the store and get you one.' Plantation store, you know. He had that charged to his account.

"I used to study my lesson. I turned the whole class down once. It was a class in spelling. I turned the class down on publication—p-u-b-l-i-c-a-t-i-o-n. They couldn't spell that. But I'll tell the world they could spell it the next day.

"My teacher had a great big crocus sack, and when she got tired of whipping them, she would put them in the sack. She never did put me in that sack one time. I got a whipping most every day. I used to fight, and when I wasn't fightin' for myself I'd be fighting for other children that would be scared to fight for theirselves, and I'd do their fighting for them.

"That whippin' in your hand is the worst thing you ever got. Brother, it hurts. I put a teacher in jail that'd whip one of my children in the hand.

"My mama said I was six years old when the war ended and that I was born on the first day of October. During the war, I run up and down the yard and played, and run up and down the street and played. And when I would make too much noise, they'd whip me and send me back to my mother and tell her not to whip me no more because they had already done it. I would help look after my mother's children. There were five children younger than I was. Everywhere she went, the white people would want me to nurse their children because they said, 'That little rawboned one is goin' to be the smartest one you got. I want her.' And my ma would say, 'You ain't goin' to get her.' She had two other girls—Martha and Sarah. They was older than me, and she would hire them out to do nursing. They worked for their master during slave time, and they worked for money after slavery.

"My mama's first husband was killed in a rasslin' [wrestling] match. It used to be that one man would walk up to another and say, 'You ain't no good.' And the other one would say, 'All right, let's see.' And they would rassle.

"My mother's first husband was pretty old. His name was Myers. A young man come up to him one Sunday morning when they were gettin' commodities. They got sorghum, meat, meal, and flour. If what they got wasn't enough, then they would go out and steal a hog. Sometime, they'd steal it anyhow; they got tired of eatin' the same thing all the time. Hurt would whip them for it. Wouldn't let the overseer whip them. Whip them hisself. 'Fraid the overseer wouldn't give them enough. They never could find my grandfather's meat. That was Grandfather William Down. They couldn't find his meat because he kept it hidden in a hole in the ground. It was under the floor of the cabin.

"Old Myers made this young man rassle with him. The young fellow didn't want to rassle with him; he said Myers was too old. Myers wasn't my father; he was my mother's first husband. The young man threw him. Myers wasn't satisfied with that. He wanted to rassle again. The young man didn't want to rassle again. But Myers made him. And the second time, the young man threw him so hard that he broke his collarbone. My mother was in a family way at the time. He lived about a week after that and died before the baby was born.

"My mother's second husband was named Fred Williams, and he was my father. All this was in slavery time. I am his oldest child. He raised all his children and all his stepchildren, too. He and my mother lived together for over forty years, until she was more than seventy. He was much younger than she was— just eighteen years old when he married her. And she was a woman with five children. But she was a real wife to him. Him and her would fight, too. She was jealous of him. Wouldn't be none of that with me. Honey, when you hit me once, I'm gone. Ain't no beatin' on me and then sleepin' in the same bed with you. But they fit [fought] and then they lived together right on. No matter what happened, his clean clothes were ready whenever he got ready to go out of the house, even if it was just to go to work. His meals were ready whenever he got ready to eat. They were happy together till she died. But when she died, he killed hisself courtin'. He was a young preacher. He died of pneumonia. He was visiting his daughter and got exposed to the weather and didn't take care of hisself.

"Right after the war, I was hired as a half-a-hand. After that, I got larger and was hired as a whole hand, me and the oldest girl. I worked on one farm and then another for years. I married the first time when I was fifteen years old. That was almost right after slave time. Four couples of us were married at the same time. They lived close to me. I didn't want my husband to get in the bed with me when I married the first time. I didn't have no sense. I was a Christian girl.

"Frank Sampson was his name. It rained the day we married. I got my feet wet. My husband brought me home, and then he turned round and went back to where the wedding was. They had a reception, and they danced and had a good time. Sampson could dance, too, but I didn't. A little before day, he come back and said to me—I was layin' in the middle of the bed—'Get over.' I called to Mother and told her he wanted to get in the bed with me. She said, 'Well, let him get in. He's your husband now.'

"Frank Sampson and me lived together about twenty years before he got killed, and then I married Andrew Jackson. He had children and grandchildren. I don't know what was the matter with old man Jackson. He was head deacon of the church. We only stayed together a year or more.

"I have been single ever since 1923, just bumming round white folks and tryin' to work for them and makin' them give me somethin' to eat. I ain't been tryin' to find no man. When I can't find no cookin' and washin' and ironin' to do, I used to farm. I can't farm now, and course I can't get no work to do to amount to nothin'. They say I'm too old to work.

"The welfare helps me. Don't know what I'd do if it wasn't for them. I get some commodities, too, but I don't get any wood. Some people says they pay house rent, but they never paid none of mine. I had to go to Marianna and get my application straight before I could get any help. They charged me half a dollar to fix out the application. The welfare wanted to know how I got the money to pay for the application if I didn't have money to live on. I had to get it, and I had to get the money to go to Marianna, too. If I hadn't, I never would have got no help.

"I told you my first husband got killed. The mule run away with his plow and throwed him a summerset [somersault]. His head was where his heels should have been, he said, and the mule dragged him. His chest was crushed and mashed. His face was cut and dirtied. He lived nine days and a half after he was hurt and couldn't eat one grain of rice. I never left his bedside 'cept to cook a little broth for him. That's all he would eat—just a little broth.

"He said to his friend, 'See this little woman of mine? I hate to leave her. She's just such a good little woman. She ain't got no business in this world without a husband.' And his friend said to him, 'Well, you might as well make up your mind you got to leave her, 'cause you goin' to do it.'

"He got hurt on Thursday, and I couldn't get a doctor till Friday. Dr. Harper, the plantation doctor, had got his house burned and his hands hurt. So he couldn't come out to help us. Finally, Dr. Hodges come. He come from Sunnyside, Mississippi, and he charge me fourteen dollars. He just made two trips, and he didn't do nothin'.

"Bowls and pitchers were in style then. And I always kept a pitcher of clean water in the house. I looked up and there was a bunch of men comin' in the house. It was near dark then. They brought Sampson in and carried him to the bed and put him down. I said, 'What's the matter with Frank?' And they said, 'The mule drug him.' And they put him on the bed and went on out. I dipped a handkerchief in the water and wet it and put it in his mouth and took out great gobs of dust where the mule had drug him in the dirt. They didn't nobody help me with him then; I was there alone with him.

"I started to go for the doctor, but he called me back and said it wasn't no use for me to go. Couldn't get the doctor then, and if I could he'd charge too much and wouldn't be able to help him none nohow. So we wasn't able to get the doctor till the next day, and then it wasn't the plantation doctor. We had planted fifteen acres in cotton, and we had ordered five hundred pounds of meat for our winter supply and laid it up. But Frank never got to eat none of it. They sent three or four hands over to get their meals with me, and they ate up all the meat and all the other supplies we had. I didn't want it. It wasn't no use to me when Frank was gone. After they paid the doctor's bill and took out for the supplies we was supposed to get, they handed me thirty-three dollars and thirty-five cents. That was all I got out of fifteen acres of cotton.

"I sew with ravelin's. Here is some ravelin's I use. I pull that out of tobacco sacks, flour sacks, anything. When I don't have the money to buy a spool of thread, I sew right on just as good with the ravelin's as if it was thread. Tobacco sacks make the best ravelin's. I got two bags full of tobacco sacks that I ain't unraveled yet. There is a man downtown who saves them for me.

When a man pulls out a sack, he says, 'Save that sack for me. I got an old colored lady that makes thread out of tobacco sacks.' These is what he has give me. [She showed the interviewer a sack which had fully a gallon of little tobacco sacks in it.]

"They didn't use ravelin's in slave time. They spun the thread. Then they balled it. Then they twisted it, and then they sew with it. They didn't use ravelin's then, but they used them right after the war.

"My mama used to say, 'Come here, Lugenia.' She and me would work together. She wanted me to reel for her. Ain't you never seen these reels? They turn like a spinning wheel, but it is made different. You turn till the thing pops, then you tie it, then it's ready to go to the loom. It is in hanks after it leaves the reel, and it is pretty, too.

"I used to live in a four-room house. They charged me seven dollars and a half a month for it. They fixed it all up and then they wanted to charge ten dollars, and it wouldn't have been long before they went up to fifteen. So I moved. This place ain't so much. I pays five dollars and a half for it. When it rains, I have to go outside to keep from gettin' too wet. But I cut down the weeds all around the place. I planted some flowers in the front yard and some vegetables in the back. That all helps me out.

"When I go to get commodities, I walk to the place. I can't stand the way these people act on the cars [streetcars]. Of course, when I have a bundle, I have to use the car to come back. I just put it on my head and walk down to the car line and get on. Lord, my mother used to carry some bundles on her head."

Julia "Aunt Sally" Brown

Born: 1852
Age: Eighty-five
Master: Nash
Place: Jackson County, Georgia
Interviewer: Geneva Tonsill
Source: First Series, Library of Congress Rare Book Room
Collection, Georgia Narratives, volume 12A, page 141

Aunt Sally rocked back and forth incessantly. She mopped her wrinkled face with a dirty rag as she talked.

"Ah was born four miles from Commerce, Georgia, and was thirteen year old at surrender. Ah belonged to the Nash fambly—three ol'-maid sisters. My mama belonged to the Nashes, and my papa belonged to General Burns; he was a officer in the war. There was six of us chilluns—Lucy, Malvina, Johnnie, Callie, Joe, and me. We didn't stay together long, as we was give out to different people. The Nashes didn't believe in selling slaves, but we was known as their niggers. They sold one once 'cause the other slaves said they would kill him 'cause he had a baby by his own daughter. So to keep him from bein' kilt, they sold him.

"My mama died the year of surrender. Ah didn't fare well after her death. Ah had such a hard time. Ah was give to the Mitchell fambly, and they done every cruel thing they could to me. Ah slept on the floor nine years, winter and summer, sick or well. Ah never wore anything but a cotton dress, a shimmy, and drawers. That woman didn't care what happened to the niggers. Sometime, she would take us to church. We'd walk to the church house. Ah never went nowhere else. That woman took delight in sellin' slaves. She'd lash us with a cowhide whip. Ah had to shift for myself.

"They didn't mind the slaves matin', but they wanted their niggers to marry only amongst them on their place. They didn't 'low 'em to mate with other slaves from other places. When the women had babies, they was treated kind, and they let 'em stay in. We called it 'lay-in,' just about like they do now. We didn't go to no hospitals as they do now. We just had our babies and had a granny to catch 'em. We didn't have all the pain-easin' medicines then. The granny would put a rusty piece of tin or an ax under the mattress, and this would ease the pains. The granny put an ax under my mattress once. This was to stop the after-pains, and she did it, too, honey. We'd set up the fifth day, and after the layin'-in time was up we was 'lowed to walk outdoors, and they told us to walk around the house just once and come in the house. This was to keep us from takin' a 'lapse.

"We wasn't 'lowed to go around and have pleasure as the folks does today. We had to have passes to go wherever we wanted. When we'd get out, there was a bunch of white man called the 'pattyrollers.' They'd come in and see if all us had passes, and if they found any who didn't have a pass he was whipped, give fifty or more lashes—and they'd count the lashes. If they said a hundred, you got a hundred. They was somethin' like the Ku Klux. We was 'fraid to tell our masters about the pattyrollers because we was scared they'd whip us again, for we was told not to tell. They'd sing a little ditty. Ah wish Ah could remember the words, but it went somethin' like this: 'Run, niggah, run, de pattyrollers'll get you. Run, niggah, run, you'd better get away.'

"We was 'fraid to go any place.

"Slaves were treated in most cases like cattle. A man went about the country buyin' up slaves like buyin' up cattle and the like, and he was called a speculator, then he'd sell 'em to the highest bidder. Oh! It was pitiful to see chillun taken from their mothers' breast, mothers sold, husbands sold from wives. One woman he was to buy had a baby. Of course, the baby come befo' he bought her, and he wouldn't buy the baby, said he hadn't bargained to buy the baby, too, and he just wouldn't.

"My uncle was married, but he was owned by one master and his wife was owned by another. He was 'lowed to visit his wife on Wednesday and Saturday—that's the onliest time he could get off. He went one Wednesday, and when he went back on Saturday his wife had been bought by the speculator, and he never did know where she was.

"Ah worked hard always. Honey, you can't 'magine what a hard time Ah had. Ah split rails like a man. How did Ah do it? Ah used a huge glut—an iron wedge drove into the wood with a maul—and this would split the wood.

"Ah help spin the cotton into thread for our clothes. After the thread was made, we used a loom to weave the cloth. We had no sewin' machines, had to sew by hand. My mistress had a big silver bird, and she would always catch the cloth in the bird's bill, and this would hold it for her to sew.

"Ah didn't get to handle money when I was young. Ah worked from sunup to sundown. We never had overseers like some of the slaves. We was give so much work to do in a day, and if the white folks went off on a vacation they would give us so much work to do while they was gone, and we better have all of that done, too, when they'd come home. Some of the white folks was very kind to their slaves. Some did not believe in slavery, and some freed them befo' the war and even give 'em land and homes. Some would give the niggers meal, lard, and like that. They made me hoe when Ah was a chile, and Ah'd keep right up with the others, 'cause they'd tell me that if Ah got behind, a runaway nigger would get me and split open my head and get the milk outen it. Of course, Ah didn't know then that wasn't true. Ah believed everything they told me, and that made me work the harder.

"There was a white man, Mr. Jim, that was very mean to the slaves. He'd go round and beat 'em. He'd even go to the little homes, tear down the chimneys, and do all sorts of cruel things. The chimneys was made of mud an' straw an' sticks; they was powerful strong, too. Mr. Jim was just a mean man, and when he died we all said God got tired of Mr. Jim being so mean and kilt him. When they laid him out on the coolin' board, everybody was settin' round moanin' over his death, and all of a sudden Mr. Jim rolled offen the coolin' board, and such a runnin' and gettin' outen that room you never saw. We said Mr. Jim was tryin' to run the niggers, and we was 'fraid to go about at night. Ah believed it then. Now that they's embalmin', Ah know that must have been gas and he was purgin', for they didn't know nothin' 'bout embalmin' then. They didn't keep dead folks outen the ground long in them days.

"Doctors wasn't so plentiful then. They'd go round in buggies and on hosses. Them that rode on a hoss had saddle pockets just filled with little bottles, and lots of them. He'd try one medicine, and if it didn't do no good he'd try another until it did do good, and when the doctor went to see a sick person he'd stay right there until he was better. He didn't just come in and write a 'scription for somebody to take to a drugstore. We used herbs a lots in them days. When a body had dropsy, we'd set him in a tepid bath made of mullein leaves. There was a jimson weed we'd use for rheumatism, and for asthma we'd use tea made of chestnut leaves. We'd sit the chestnut leaves, dry them in the sun just like leaves, and we wouldn't let them leaves get wet for nothin' in the world while they was dryin'. We'd take poke-salad roots, boil them, and then take sugar and make a syrup. This was the best thing for asthma. It was known to cure it, too. For colds and such, we used horehound, made candy outen it with brown sugar. We used whiskey for colds, too. They had a remedy that they used for consumption—take dry cow manure, make a tea of this and flavor it with mint and give it to the sick person. We didn't need many doctors then for we didn't have so much sickness in them days, and naturally they didn't die so fast; folks lived a long time then. They used a lot of peach-tree leaves, too, for fever, and when the stomach got upset we'd crush the leaves, pour water over them, and wouldn't let them drink any other kind of water till they was better. Ah still believes in them ol' homemade medicines, too, and Ah don't believe in so many doctors.

"We didn't have stoves plentiful them, just fireplaces. Ah's toted many an armful of bark—good ol' hickory bark to cook with. We'd cook light bread, both flour and corn. The yeast for this bread was made from hops. Coals of fire was put on top of the oven and under the bottom, too. Everything was cooked on coals from a wood fire—coffee and all. Wait, let me show you my coffee trivet. Have you ever seen one? Well, Ah'll show you mine."

Aunt Sally got up and hobbled to the kitchen to get the trivet. After a few moments' search, she came back into the room.

"No, it's not there. Ah guess it's been put in the basement. Ah'll show it to you when you come back. It's a rack made of iron that the pot is set on befo' puttin' it on the fire coals. The victuals was good in them days. We got our vegetables outen the garden in season and didn't have all the hothouse vegetables. Ah don't eat many vegetables now unless they come outen the garden and I know it.

"Well, as I said, there was racks fitted in the fireplace to put pots on. Once, there was a big pot settin' on the fire, just boilin' away with a big roast in it. As the water boiled, the meat turned over and over, comin' up to the top and goin' down again. Ol' Sandy the dog come in the kitchen. He sat there awhile and watched that meat roll over and over in the pot, and all of a sudden-like he grabbed at that meat and pulls it outen the pot. Course, he couldn't eat it 'cause it was hot, and they got the meat befo' he et it. The kitchen was away from the big house, so the victuals was cooked and carried up to the house. Ah'd carry it up myself. We didn't eat all the different victuals the white folks et, and one mornin' when I was carryin' the big pot to the big home we had waffles that was a pretty golden brown and pipin' hot. They was a picture to look at, and Ah just couldn't keep from takin' one, and that was the hardest waffle for me to eat befo' Ah got to the big home. Ah just couldn't get rid of that waffle 'cause my conscience whipped me so.

"They taught me to do everything. Ah'd use battlin' blocks and battlin' sticks to wash the clothes; we all did. On most days, you could hear then battlin' sticks poundin' every which way. We made our own soap, used ol' meat and grease, and poured water over wood ashes which was kept in a rack-like thing, and the water would drip through the ashes. This made strong lye. We used a lot o' such lye, too, to bile with.

"Sometimes, the slaves would run away. Their masters was mean to them. That caused them to run away. Sometimes, they would live in caves. How did they get along? Well, chile, they got along all right, what with other people slippin' things in to 'em. And, too, they'd steal hogs, chickens, and anything else they could get their hands on. Some white people would help, too, for there was some white people who didn't believe in slavery. Yes, they'd try to find them slaves that run away, and if they was found they'd be beat or sold to somebody else. My grandmother run away from her master. She stayed in the woods, and she washed her clothes in the branches. She use sand for soap. Yes, chile, I reckon they got 'long all right in the caves. They had babies in there and raised 'em, too.

"Ah stayed with the Mitchells till Miss Hannah died. Ah even helped to lay her out. Ah didn't go to the graveyard, though. Ah didn't have a home after she died, and Ah wandered from place to place, stayin' with a white fambly this time and then a nigger fambly the next time. Ah moved to Jackson County and stayed with a Mr. Frank Dowdy. Ah didn't stay there long, though. Then Ah moved to Winder, Georgia. They called it 'Jug Tavern' in them days 'cause jugs was made there. Ah married Green Hinton in Winder. Got along well after marryin' him. He farmed for a livin' and made a good livin' for me and the eight chillun, all born in Winder. The chillun was grown nearly when he died and was able to help me with the smallest ones. Ah got along all right after his death and didn't have such a hard time raisin' the chilluns. Then Ah married Jim Brown and moved to Atlanta. Jim farmed at first for a livin', and then he worked on the railroad—the Seaboard. He helped to grade the first railroad track for that line. He was a sand dryer."

Aunt Sally broke off her story here. "Lord, honey, Ah got such a pain in my stomach Ah don't believe Ah can go on. It's a gnawin' kind o' pain. Just keeps me weak all over." Naturally, I suggested that we complete the story at another time. So I left, promising to return in a few days. A block from the house, I stepped in a store to order some groceries for Aunt Sally. The proprietor, a Jewish woman, spoke up when I gave the delivery address. She explained in broken English that she knew Aunt Sally: "I think you was very kind to do dis for Aunt Sally. She needs it. I often give her some food. Her son passes here yesterday, and he look so wasted and hungry. His stomach look like it was drawn in, you know. I give him some fresh hocks. I was trained to help people in need. It's part of my religion. See, if ve sit on de streetcar and an old person comes in and finds no seat, we get up and gif him one. If ve see a person loaded vid bundles and he is old and barely able to go, ve gif a hand. See, ve Jews, you colored, but ve know no difference. Anyone needing help, ve gif."

A couple of days later, I was back at Aunt Sally's. I had brought some groceries for the old woman. I knocked a long time on the front door and, getting no answer, I picked my way through the rank growth of weeds and grass surrounding the house and went around to the back door. It opened into the kitchen, where Aunt Sally and her son were having breakfast. The room was small and dark, and I could hardly see the couple, but Aunt Sally welcomed me.

"Land, honey, you come right on in. I told John I heard somebody knockin' at the door."

"You been hearin' things all mornin'," John spoke up. He turned to me. "You must've been thinkin' about Mama just when we started eatin' breakfast because she asked me did I hear somebody call her. I told her the Lawd

Jesus is always a-callin' poor niggers, but she said it sounded like the lady's voice who was here the other day. Well, I didn't hear anything, and I told her she must be hearin' things."

I'd put the bag of groceries on the table unobtrusively, but Aunt Sally wasn't one to let such gifts pass unnoticed. Eagerly, she tore the bag open and began pulling out the packages.

"Lawd bless you, chile, and He sho will bless you! I feels rich seein' what you brought me. Just look at this— Lawdy mercy!—rolls, butter, milk, baloney. Oh, this baloney, just looky there! You musta knowed what I wanted! And those eggs! Honey, you knows God is goin' to bless you and let you live long. Ah's goin' to cook one at a time. And Ah been wantin' some milk. Ah's gonna cook me a hoecake right now."

She went about putting the things in little cans and placing them on shelves or in the dilapidated little cupboard that stood in a corner. I sat down near the door and listened while she rambled on.

"Ah used to say young people didn't care 'bout ol' folks, but Ah is takin' that back now. Ah just told my son the other day that it's turned round. The young folks thinks of the ol' and tries to help 'em, and the ol' folks don't try to think of each other. Some of them, they is too mean. Ah can't understand it. Ah just know I heard you call me when Ah started to eat, and tell my son so. Ah sho did enjoy the victuals you sent day before yistidy. They send me surplus food from the gov'ment, but Ah don't like what they send. The skim milk gripes me, and Ah don't like that yellow meal. A friend brought me some white meal the other day. And that wheat cereal they send! Ah eats it with water when

Ah don't have milk, and Ah don't like it, but when you don't have nothin' else you got to eat what you have. They send me seventy-five cents every two weeks, but that don't get very far. Ah ain't complainin', for Ah'm thankful for what Ah get.

"They send a girl to help me around the house, too. She's from the housekeepin' department. She's very nice to me. Yes, she sholy is a sweet girl, and her foreman is sweet, too. She comes in now an' then to see me. She washes, too. Ah's been on relief a long time. When Ah first got on it, they give me plenty of anything Ah asked for, and my visitor was Mrs. Tompkins. She was so good to me. Well, they stopped that, and then the DPW [Department of Public Welfare] took care of me. When they first started, Ah got more than I do now, and they've cut me down till Ah gets only a mighty little.

"Yes, Ah was talkin' about my husband when you was here the other day. He was killed on the railroad. After he moved here, he bought this home. Ah's lived here twenty years. Jim was comin' in the railroad yard one day and stepped off the little engine they used for the workers right in the path of the L&H train. He was cut up and crushed to pieces. He didn't have a sign of a head. They used a rake to get up the pieces they did get. A man brought a few pieces out here in a bundle, and Ah wouldn't even look at them.

"Ah got a little money from the railroad, but the lawyer got most of it. He brought me a few dollars out and told me not to discuss it with anyone, nor tell how much Ah got. Ah tried to get some of the men that worked with him to tell me just how it all happened, but they wouldn't talk. Them niggers held their peace and wouldn't tell me anything. The bossman come out later, but he didn't seem interested in it at all, so Ah got little or nothing for his death. The lawyer got it for hisself.

"All my chilluns died 'cept my son, and he is ol' and sick

and can't do nothin' for me or hisself. He gets relief, too, seventy-five cents every two weeks. He goes round and people gives him a little to eat. We has a hard time tryin' to get 'long.

"Ah had a double bed in the other room and let a woman have it so she could get some of the delegates to the Baptist World Alliance, and she was goin' to pay me for lettin' her use the bed, but she didn't get anybody 'cept two. They came there on Friday and left the next day. She was told that lots of people went to the expense to prepare for them and didn't get a one. Ah was sorry, for Ah intended to use what she paid me for my water bill. Ah owes five dollars and had to give my deeds to my house to a lady to pay the water bill for me, and it worries me 'cause Ah ain't got no money to pay it, for this is all Ah got, and Ah hates to lose my house. Ah wish it was some way to pay it. Ah ain't been able to do for myself in many years now, and has to depend on what others gives me.

"Tell you mo' about the ol' times? Lawd, honey, times has changed so from when Ah was young. You don't hear of haints as you did when I growed up. The Lawd had to show His work in miracles 'cause we didn't have learnin' in them days as they has now. And you may not believe it, but them things happened. Ah knows a old man what died, and after his death he would come to our house, where he always cut weed, and at night we could hear a chain bein' drug along in the yard, just as if a big log chain was bein' pulled by somebody. It would drag on up to the woodpile and stop, then we could hear the *thump-thump* of the ax on the wood. The woodpile was near the chimney, and it would *chop-chop* on, then stop, and we could hear the chain bein' drug back the way it come. This went on for several nights until my father got tired, and one night after he heard it so long, the *chop-chop*, Papa got mad and hollered at the haint, 'G— d--- you, go to hell!' and that spirit went off and never did come back!

"We'd always know somebody was goin' to die when we heard a owl come to a house and start screechin'. We always said, 'Somebody is gwine to die!' Honey, you don't hear it now, and it's good you don't, for it would scare you to death nearly. It sounded so mournful-like, and we'd put the poker or the shovel in the fire, and that always run him away; it burned his tongue out, and he couldn't holler no more. If they'd let us go out like we always wanted to, Ah don't 'spect we'd of done it, 'cause we was too scared. Lawdy, chile, them was tryin' days. Ah sho is glad God let me live to see these ones.

"Ah tried to get the ol'-age pension, for Ah sholy needed it and was 'titled to it, too. Sho was. But that visitor just wouldn't let me go through. She acted like that money belonged to her. Ah 'plied when it first come out and shoulda been one of the first to get one. Ah worried powerful much at first, for Ah felt how much better off Ah'd be. Ah wouldn't be so dependent like Ah is now. Ah 'spect you knows that woman. She is a big black woman, was named Smith at first befo' she married. She is a Johns now. She sho is a mean woman. She just wouldn't do no way. Ah even told her if she let me go through and Ah got my pension, Ah would give her some of the money Ah got, but she just didn't do no way. She told me if Ah was put on Ah'd get no more than Ah was gettin'. Ah sho believes them that's on gets more than seventy-five cents every two weeks. Ah sho had a hard time and a rough road to travel with her my visitor until they sent in the housekeeper, for she just went right out and got me some clothes. Everything Ah needed. When Ah told her how my visitor was doin' me, she just went out and come right back with all the things Ah needed. Ah don't know why my visitor done me like that. Ah said at first it was because I had this house, but honey, what could Ah do with a house when Ah was hungry and not able to work? Ah always worked hard. Course,

Ah didn't get much for it, but Ah like to work for what Ah gets."

Aunt Sally was beginning to repeat herself, and I began to suspect she was talking just to please me. So I arose to go.

"Lawdy mercy, chile, you sho is sweet to set here and talk to a ol' woman like me. Ah sho is glad you come. Ah told my son you was a bundle of sunshine, and Ah felt so much better the day you left—and here you is again! Chile, my nose wasn't itchin' for nothin'! You come back to see me real soon. Ah's always glad to have you. And the Lawd's gonna sho go with you for bein' so good to me."

My awareness of the obvious fulsomeness in the old woman's praise in no way detracted from my feeling of having done a good deed. Aunt Sally was a clever psychologist, and as I carefully picked my way up the weedy path toward the street I felt indeed that the "Lawd" was "sho goin' " with me.

EMMALINE KILPATRICK

Born: 1863
Age: Seventy-four
Master: William Moore
Place: Greene County, Georgia
Interviewer: Sarah H. Hall
Source: First Series, Library of Congress Rare Book Room
Collection, Georgia Narratives, volume 13A, page 8

One morning in October, as I finished planting hyacinth bulbs on my cemetery lot, I saw an old Negro woman approaching. She was Emmaline Kilpatrick, born in 1863 on my grandfather's plantation.

"Mornin', Miss Sarah," she began, "Ah seed ya out here in de graveyard, an' I come right over for to get ya to read yo' aunt Willie's birthday offen her tombstone an' put it in writin' for me."

"I don't mind doing that for you, Emmaline," I replied, "but why do you want to know my aunt's birthday?"

"Well," answered the old ex-slave, "I can't rightly tell my age no other way. My mammy, she told me I was borned de same night as Miss Willie was, an' Mammy allus told me iffen I ever want to know how ol' I is, just ask my white folks how ol' Miss Willie is."

When I had penciled the birth date on a scrap of paper torn from my notebook and she had tucked it carefully away in a pocket in her clean blue-checked gingham apron, Emmaline began to talk of the old days on my grandfather's farm.

"Miss Sarah, Ah sho did love yo' aunt Willie. We was chilluns growin' up together on Marse Billie's place. You might not know it, but black chilluns gets grown heap faster dan white chilluns, an' whilst us played round de yard an' orchards an' pastures out dere, I was 'sposed to take care of Miss Willie an' not let her get hurt, er nothin' happen to her.

"My mammy say dat when Marse Billie come home from de war, he call all his niggers together an' tell 'em dey is free an' don't belong to nobody no mo'. He say dat any of 'em dat want to can go 'way and live where dey likes an' do like dey want to. Howsomever, he do say iffen anybody wants to stay wid him an' live right on in de same cabins, dey can do it iffen dey promise him to be good niggers an' mind him like dey allus done.

"Most all de niggers stayed wid Marse Billie, 'ceppen two or three brash good-for-nothin's."

Standing there in the cemetery, as I listened to old Emmaline tell of the old days, I could see cotton being loaded on freight cars at the depot. I asked Emmaline to tell what she could remember of the days when we had no railroad to haul the cotton to market.

"Well," she said, " 'fore dis here railroad was made, dey hauled de cotton to de Point [Union Point] an' sold it dere. De Point's just 'bout twelve miles from here. 'Fore dey had a railroad through de Point, Marse Billie used to haul his cotton clear down to Jewell to sell it. My mammy say dat long 'fore de war, he used to wait till all de cotton was picked in de fall, an' den he would have it all loaded on his wagons. Not long 'fore sundown, he would start de wagons off, wid yo' uncle Anderson bossin' 'em, on de all-night-long ride towards Jewell. 'Bout four in de mornin', Marse Billie an' yo' grammaw Miss Margie would start off in de surrey, driving de bays, an' 'fore dem wagons get to Jewell Marse Billie done catch up wid 'em. He drive ahead an' lead 'em on to de cotton mill in Jewell, where he sell all his cotton. Den him an' Miss Margie, dey go to de mill store an' buy white sugar an' other things dey don't raise on de plantation, an' load 'em on de wagons an' start back home."

"But Emmaline," I interrupted, "Sherman's army passed through Jewell and burned the houses and destroyed the property there. How did the people market their cotton then?"

Emmaline scratched her head. "Ah 'members somethin' 'bout dat," she declared. "Yes'm, I sho does 'member my mammy sayin' dat folks said when de Federals was burnin' up everything 'bout Jewell dey was settin' fire to de mill, when de boss of dem soldiers look up an' see a sign up over every upstairs window. It was de Masons' sign up dere 'cause dat was de Masons' lodge, held up over de mill. De soldier boss, he makes de other soldiers put out de fire. He say him a Mason hisself, an he ain't gwine see nobody burn up a Masonic hall. Dey kinda tears up some of de fixin's at de mill works, but dey didn't burn down de mill house, 'cause he ain't let 'em do nothin' to de Masonic hall. Ya knows, Miss Sarah, Ah was just 'bout two years ol' when dat happen, but I ain't heared nothin' 'bout no time when dey didn't take cotton to Jewell every year till de railroad come here.

"Did ya ask me who married my maw an' paw? Why, Marse Billie did! He was Judge Moore, Marse Billie was, an' he won't gwine have no foolishment 'mongst his niggers. 'Fore de war an' durin' de war, de niggers went to de same church where dere white folks went. Only de niggers, dey set in de gallery. Marse Billie made all his niggers work mighty hard, but he sho took good care of 'em. Miss Margie allus made 'em send for her when de chilluns was borned in de slave cabins. My mammy, she say I's 'bout de onliest slave baby Miss Margie didn't look after de bornin', on dat plantation. When a nigger on dat farm was sick, Marse Billie seed dat he had medicine an' lookin' after, an' if he was bad sick Marse Billie had de white folks' doctor come see 'bout him.

"Did us have shoes? Yes, ma'am, us had shoes. Dat was all ol' Pegleg was good for, just to make shoes an' fix shoes after dey was 'bout to give out. Pegleg made de everyday shoes for Marse Billie's own chilluns, 'cept now an' then Marse Billie fetched 'em home some store-bought shoes from Jewell.

"Yes'm, us sho was scared of ghosts. Dem days when de war won't long gone, niggers sho was scared of graveyards. Most every nigger kept a rabbit foot, 'cause ghosties ain't gwine bother nobody that had a left hind foot from a graveyard rabbit. Dem days, dere was most allus woods round de graveyards, an' it was easy to catch a rabbit as he loped out of de graveyard. Lawsy, Miss Sarah, those days Ah sho wouldn't of been standin' here in no graveyard talkin' to anybody, even in wide-open daytime.

"An' you ask was dey anything else us was scared of? Yes'm, us allus did get mighty uneasy if a screech owl hollered at night. Pappy would hop right out of his bed an' stick de fire shovel in de coals. Iffen he did dat right quick, an' look over his left shoulder whilst de shovel gettin' hot, den maybe no nigger gwine die dat week on dat plantation. An' us never did like to find a hoss tail hair in de hoss trough, 'cause us was sho to meet a snake 'fore long.

"Yes'm, us had charms for a heap of things. Us got 'em from a ol' Injun woman dat lived 'cross de creek. Her sold us charms to make de mens like us, an' charms dat would get a boy baby, an' another kind of charm iffen you want a gal baby. Miss Margie allus scold 'bout de charms an' make us 'shamed to wear 'em, 'cept she don't mind if us wear aserfitidy [asafetida] charms to keep off fevers, an' she don't say nothin' when my mammy wear nutmeg on a wool string round her neck to keep off de rheumatiz.

"Is you got to get on home now, Miss Sarah? Lemme tote dat hoe an' trowel to de car for ya. You gwine take me home in your car wid ya, so as I can weed your flower garden? Yes'm, I sho will be proud to do it for de black dress you wore last year. Ah gwine to get every speck of grass out of yo' flowers, 'cause ain't you just like yo' grammaw, my Miss Margie."

SLAVERY COOKING

Born: Various
Age: Various
Master: Various
Place: Warren County, Mississippi
Interviewer: Lois Lawrence
Source: First Supplemental Series, Mississippi Narratives,
    volume 10S, page 1961

Tilda Johnson relates that during slavery, cooking was considered a very light and easy job. Any slave woman who was
allowed to stay at the house and manage the pots and pans was
almost a favorite, as only neat, clean, and careful women were
selected for the job of cooking in those days. Sometimes, the
cook had many helpers, but often when field work became rushed
one woman would have to manage to carry on, and that meant
not only to cook the meals but churn the butter and bring
water from the spring, nearly a mile away. Tilda lived on a
large plantation and handled the job of cooking. "I was a gal of
fourteen, but I could do a woman's work," said Tilda. "I knew
how to wash, iron, clean up, and cook, but my job was to cook,
so I never went to the fields. I was often abused by de other
slaves and called 'old puffed-up house rat.' I wasn't a house rat,
though, as I used to get out and chop wood, pick up chips and

pine burs to make my fire burn fast, [and] bring three pails of water up the hill from the spring, one on my head and one in each hand. I knew how to cook good, plain food, and at holiday time I cooked plenty pastry and other goodies."

A plain dinner consisted of plenty of boiled meat, greens, beans, cornbread, milk, and butter, and sometimes game or fish.

"My marster's favorite bread was ashcakes, and this is how it was made. A quart of meal, salt, soda, sour milk, and a few spoons of sorghum molasses make a stiff pone that can be handled easily. Clean hearth with a rag. Place pone on the hot hearth and let it stand under the heat until a light crust forms, cover with ashes, and cook until a smoke rises from the ashes. Remove from fire, brush off ashes, and wipe with a damp cloth. Many is de time when I has served my marster ashcake, butter, and cold buttermilk in de kitchen, and dere was plenty of everything good on de big table," said Tilda. "When dey had guests, dey really put on de dog. I used to roast little pigs whole. First, rub pomegranate juice all over de meat [and] make a dressing of stale bread, hickory nuts, and chicker pins [chinquapin nuts]. Sprinkle salt, pepper, and flour over it. Put little pieces of butter all over it and put him in de old clay oven to brown. And when I'd take dat little rascal out, you could smell him a mile. Den I'd lay him on a big platter, place an apple in his mouth, lay some molds of hog's-foot jelly round him, and he'd be ready for de table. A lot of times, de white gals who was too 'shame to eat a heap at de table would come out to talk to me and eat a heap more dan I could."

"You didn't ever hear of cooking make nobody sick in dem days, lessen dey ate too much," said Marry Joiner. Marry used to cook for officers in the Confederate army. When asked what she liked to cook best, Marry replied, "Chicken, but one of de officers used to like a dumplin' cooked in a bag. Roll out dough as if for a pie, put in fruit [berries], roll these in the dough, put in a bag, and boil in water. When this is done, serve with a sauce made of butter and crushed mint leaves."

For fried chicken, Marry said to "cut a chicken into large pieces, [add] salt [and] pepper, and sprinkle with lemon juice. Dredge with flour that has a few grains of sugar in it. Fry with hot butter in a covered skillet. As each piece browns, drop it into another covered skillet that has a little hot sweet milk in it. Let steam and serve."

To make greens and dumplings, "take young, tender turnip greens and remove all of the stems, wash thoroughly, put into a pot that meat, salt, an' ham hocks have been boiling in an hour, [and] put in a pod of red pepper [and] a little salt and black pepper. Let simmer an hour, remove from fire, [and] put in corn-meal dumplings, using a thin cloth between the greens and the meal dumplings. Cook until the dumplings are done. This dish is good for anybody," said Sally Green, age seventy-eight.

For persimmon loaf, "take de seed outen de 'simmon [and] cover de fruit wid sugar. Take one cup of flour and one cup of sugar to every four cups of 'simmons. Add a little butter and an egg well beaten. Bake in the oven. Slice when cold. It goes well wid meats an' makes nice sandwiches," said Millie Young of Cedar Grove, age seventy-four.

"Good eats didn't make folks sick in dem days," said Millie Boyd. "I 'members being de table girl on the Hanses' place near de river, and de table was eight feet long [and] three feet wide and was loaded wid things to eat, besides dere was more in de pantry and more in de kitchen and food a-plenty in de smokehouse. I used to love to set up a table and wait on guests. I wore a blue polka-dot dress, a wide white apron, and a white turban cap. Dere were blue dishes bought from 'cross de water, silver shining, plenty wine and mint juleps, a black boy to fan de flies away, and a big girl to help fill de glasses from de side table. Dere would be from four to six kinds of meat pies in stacks, cakes of every kind, plenty sauces and jelly, preserves, relishes, pickles—good food."

"Negroes had more better food dan dey does now," said Granny Lee of Lums Quarters. "Some of 'em brought good pans from dey big houses, and some of 'em were smart enough to hustle around and get food deyselves. Just like Clarence Franks, de man who used to kill hogs in de woods just to cut out de liver to fry. And plenty fine meat and game could be found in cabin homes." Game was plentiful, too, and squirrels were a great dish.

To make squirrel pie, "steam six squirrels till tender, remove from pot, [and] season with salt, pepper, and butter," Granny Lee said. "Make a little thickening outen flour and sweet milk. Turn a bowl in the middle of a deep pie pan, put the mixture in, and cover with a short crust of pastry. Cover pastry with butter. Put on heavy top of skillet and cook slowly in front of an open fireplace."

"Don't forget to tell her about what you can do wid a coon," said Mary Willis to her mother, Ellen Gooden of Vine Street. "Oh," said Ellen, "you don't see many coons nowadays, but den you'd catch 'em any day. I's de best coon cooker dere is when I gets me a fine, fat coon and he is dressed clean, den I rubs him all over in fine-ground red pepper, dusts him wid salt, puts just a little water in my black iron pot, and steams him 'bout two hours, takes him offen de fire, sprinkles him wid vinegar [and] a dash of sugar, puts flour, butter, [and] plenty black pepper on him, and as he browns I pour on him hot water to make plenty good brown gravy. I has my rice in anudder pot, and when dey is all done I lays a row of rice around him in a large pan or platter [and] pours de gravy over de rice. Chile, let me hush, 'cause you nor me can't stand no more of dat."

To make potato pone, "grate raw potatoes into a bowl with a beaten egg, sweet milk, butter, and a double grating of nutmeg, add one-half cup of flour and one cup of sugar or one and one-half cup of cane molasses. Put in a skillet with a flat-top cover with red-hot coals. Bake until done. This is a grand dish," said Callie Morris. "All persons in Mississippi like potato pone. Potato pone and cold sweet milk make a mighty good dinner. Sometimes, you put parched shelled peanuts in it."

Witches/Doctors

"Does I believe in witches? S-a-a-y, I knows more 'bout 'em dan to just believe. I been *rid* by one. Right here in de house. You ain't never been rid by a witch? Well, you mighty lucky. Dey come in de night, ginnerly soon after you drop off to sleep. Dey put a bridle on your head an' a bit in your mouth an' a saddle on your back. Den dey take off their skin an' hang it up on de wall. Den dey get on you, an' some nights dey like to ride you to death."

Josephine Anderson interview

Witches/Doctors

"Women have always been healers," write Barbara Ehrenreich and Deirdre English in *Witches, Midwives, and Nurses: A History of Women Healers*. "They were the unlicensed doctors and anatomists of western history. They were abortionists, nurses and counselors. They were pharmacists, cultivating healing herbs and exchanging the secrets of their uses. They were midwives, traveling from home to home and village to village. For centuries women were doctors without degrees, barred from books and lectures, learning from each other, and passing on experience from neighbor to neighbor and mother to daughter. They were called 'wise women' by the people, witches or charlatans by the authorities. Medicine is part of our heritage as women, our history, our birthright."[27]

In the nineteenth century, doctors were few and far between, and those "regular" doctors who did practice did so with a mixture of skill, theory, and a small amount of knowledge gathered from their sporadic "formal" medical training. Regular doctors saw primarily the middle and upper class, persons not unlike themselves who could afford the prestige of being treated by a "gentleman" of their own class. Custom even dictated that upper- and middle-class women employ male regular doctors for obstetrical care, a custom plainer people regarded as grossly indecent.[28] However, owners and their slaves in rural America seldom saw the likes of regular doctors. The majority of them preferred lay practitioners or were themselves skilled users of folk remedies, an area in which whites, Indians, and Africans shared certain practices and benefited from one another's knowledge.[29]

Within the enslaved community, the issue of health care was a bone of contention. At the bottom of the conflict was the question of who controlled the slaves' bodies. Masters felt that it was their place to decide the best course of action when their property was devalued, and often demanded to be informed of slaves' illnesses. The enslaved often resisted this intrusion and reacted to it in a variety of ways ranging from hiding illnesses to consulting slave healers. Herbalists, midwives, and conjurers are examples of the variety of healers on Southern plantations.[30] Much of the tendency toward trusting traditional healers came from their African background, which contributed not only specific cures but also a general world view of health and healing. According to John S. Mbiti in *African Religions and Philosophies*, healers "symbolize the hopes of society: hopes of good health, protection and security from evil forces, prosperity and good fortune, and ritual cleansing when harm or impurities have been contracted."[31] On many plantations, the white doctor was never as popular as the "granny" or midwife who brewed home remedies from roots and herbs to treat nearly every ailment.[32]

In contrast to the rigid hierarchies of Southern slave society, medicine and health care in the Old South were a free-for-all epitomized by experimentalism, skepticism, and contesting claims to scientific legitimacy. The ill turned to Thomsonian empiricism, homeopathic healing, hydropathy, Native American traditional practices, and conjure. Southerners consulted peddlers, seers, scripture, almanacs, and above all the acquired wisdom of their families, social circles, and neighborhoods. While therapies appeared to flow across social and cultural divisions, enslaved practitioners and health seekers often struggled against racial, gender, and class-based constructions of who was fit to claim the privileges of medical authority. Into this chaos and conflict stepped the women of the enslaved community, whose responsibilities for the health of the slaveholders' families as well as their own put them in a delicate position of responsibility and helped define the nature of healing authority within antebellum culture.[33]

The dependence upon midwives and "doctor women" was a critical element in the survival of enslaved women and their children. But slaveholders intruded frequently on the health practices of slaves. Enslaved persons thus struggled continuously, and sometimes in vain, with slaveholders, overseers, and white doctors for their chance to pursue their own visions of health.[34] Elder slave women tended to the health needs of many within their midst, including whites. Despite the fact that many derided their purported skills as midwives and herbalists, black healers and nurses were regarded as indispensable to the operation of plantation hospitals. Many earned the grudging reverence of their competitors in the medical field because of the efficacy of their practices and a growing respect for the value of folk remedies derived from Africa.[35]

The power of traditional healers within the enslaved community was in many cases a double-edged sword. Though they were respected, they were also greatly feared. Though midwives were valued members of the community and served women both in the birth of their children and in the upbringing, they were also responsible for ending unwanted pregnancies. As this practice was counterproductive to the economic interests of the slave owners, it was surreptitious, if not subversive.

The knowledge of plants and herbs that many slaves brought from Africa included an understanding of which of them could induce abortion. In addition, when abortifacients were not effective, practitioners knew mechanical means to deal with unwanted pregnancies.[36] It is important to understand that slave women had good reason not to carry pregnancies to full term. Their children would not really be their own but their masters' property, to be sold according to the masters' whims. That being the case, they did not want their masters to profit from the births of their children. Lastly, childbirth was very dangerous.

It was this dual nature of traditional healers as people who dealt with life and death that created a profound mystery around them. The power of conjurers in the slave community derived from their possession of powers whites could not understand. As Lawrence Levine puts it in *Black Culture and Black Consciousness: Afro-American Folk Thought from Slavery to Freedom*, "there were things they did not know, forces they could not control, areas in which slaves could act with more knowledge and authority than their masters, ways in which the powers of whites could be muted if not thwarted entirely."[37] That conjurers could heal and promote health and spiritual welfare was an established fact, and they were well respected for this power; however, herbalists and conjurers could also practice the magic arts to right wrongs or to wreak retribution upon members of the community. Potions, fortunes, and charms were valuable commodities in many slave communities. Folks respected their value and feared those who practiced the trade.

The mystery of traditional healers, especially with respect to female practitioners, led to the belief that many of them were witches. The distinction between conjurers and witches often was very slim. By their very nature, witches served to destroy harmony, to undermine the moral fiber of the community, and to act contrary to what society demanded. Witches and the fear of witchcraft arose from within the context of an enslaved community where females lived and worked in such proximity that conflict was an inevitable part of their daily lives. People believed that their adversaries used magic to assume power or gain revenge and that sorcery was at the root of any accident, illness, ailment, or restless night.[38] No one within the community was viewed with greater fear and suspicion than those perceived to be witches. Within the ex-slave narratives, their presence is often felt.

The first story in this section comes from Georgia. Though the place and interviewer are unknown, it bears the literary trademark of Sarah Hill, who writes as much as she allows the slaves to talk. Ma Stevens is a "root doctor" whose story is equal parts "black magic," "conjure," and "witchcraft." Whether all of this is in the eyes of the interviewer or the interviewee is clouded by the shifting frames of reference. It is worth noting that Ma Stevens was brought in by the authorities and had to stand before a judge for practicing witchcraft, at which time she demonstrated her herbal formulas. Either the charges were unclear or the proof insufficient, for she was released without facing time. She did say that she was more careful after that.

Emmaline Heard is also from Georgia, hailing from Henry County, just southeast of Atlanta. She regales readers with numerous stories she has heard about conjuring both within her community and other places. Ms. Heard was interviewed several times by Minnie Ross, an African American WPA fieldworker whose background was as a social worker in Atlanta. Ms. Ross's various notes are spread over several collections of interviews with women from Georgia entitled "Folklore (Negro)." Her compilation of stories about conjure comes from the second part of her two-part interview with Emmaline Heard, whom Ms. Ross describes thus: "To back up her belief in conjure is her appearance. She is a dark-brown-skinned woman of medium height and always wears a dirty towel on her head. The towel, which was at one time white, gives her the weird look of an old-time fortune teller."

The next story is not that of a conjurer or witch but of a midwife from Caldwell County, Kentucky, who had been practicing for some forty years up to the time of her interview. She worked with white mothers as well as black ones and had "grannied" over three hundred children; during this period, she lost only two children that were born alive. Her years of experience have made her wise; she claims she can tell the gender of a baby just by the way a pregnant mother carries it. Her story shows that she was more than a midwife; she was also an herbalist whose remedies was as important as her ability to birth children.

A common story among the enslaved communities was that of the witch who, though flesh and blood, shed her skin at sundown and became a spirit who rode the back of her unfortunate sleeper. When the evening was up, she would return to her normal state unless one was to sprinkle salt and pepper on her skin, after which she would be forced to wander as a spirit forever. In the next narrative, Josephine Anderson of Tampa, Florida, tells this myth in her own words, revealing the fear it instilled among the slave community. There were many ways to prevent a witch from riding one and, rest assured, these were all well known by the people.

Amanda Styles's narrative contains what is very much a curiosity. The witch in her story is not an enslaved person but her mother's mistress, whose husband knows nothing about her night flights. When he becomes suspicious, he decides to test what he believes to be true: "Now, her husband didn't know she was a witch, so somebody tole him he could tell by cutting off one of her limbs, so one night the wife changed to a cat, and the husband cut off her forefinger what had a ring on it. After that, de wife would keep her hand hid 'cause her finger was cut off, and she knowed her husband would find out that she was the witch." In another part of Amanda Styles's story is a variant of perhaps the most famous myth of Southern culture, made known by blues master Robert Johnson, who supposedly went to the crossroad and sold his soul to the devil to learn to play the guitar. In her version, Amanda tells of a slave who "said the devil learned him to play a banjo, and if you wanted to do anything the devil could do, go to a crossroad, walk backwards, and curse God."

MA STEVENS

Born: 1833
Age: 103
Master: Unknown
Place: Unknown
Interviewer: Unknown
Source: First Supplemental Series, Georgia Narratives,
    volume 04S, page 580

I had some difficulty finding the root doctor's house. It was
located in a Negro community, and in this particular section the
dirt streets, continuing for perhaps only two blocks and ending
abruptly in a blind alley or at the rear of a small grocery store
or a house, formed an irregular, jagged pattern. The streets were
bordered with row after row of weather-beaten one-story houses,
each one so like its neighbors that it was almost impossible to
distinguish one from another. Here and there where a blind
flapped loosely in the wind or a windowpane was missing, one
had a vacant, staring expression. The search was further complicated by the fact that numbers had long been erased from
most of the houses. Each time I stopped to make inquiries,

bandanna-adorned heads appeared from windows and doors and surveyed me suspiciously. Occasionally from a discreet distance, a low-pitched voice asked about my errand.

Sly whispers and furtive glances were exchanged when I announced that I was looking for Ma Stevens, the root doctor. She was apparently a well-known character in the settlement. Superstitious neighbors confided their knowledge of her to me in awed whispers. "Ma is a root doctor for sho," and "She sho knows plenty 'bout rootin'," they told me. I was informed that people visited her little house at all hours of the day and night and that Ma had been known to work effective cures for many who had had spells cast on them by enemies.

All of the stories were not pleasant, however, for it appeared that Ma's power could be used for evil purposes, too. One woman knew of an unfortunate man who had somehow aroused the ire of the root doctor and in consequence had had "kunjuh" [conjure] worked on him and had suffered a long, lingering illness. Day after day, the victim grew weaker and weaker until be finally died.

Even those people who claimed not to believe in Ma's ability as a root worker were careful not to speak too strongly against her. "I just keep out of her way, an' when I does see her I is careful to be very polite to her" was the common way they expressed their feelings in the matter.

I rode back and forth over the rough dirt streets, stopping every so often for additional directions. At length, the proprietor of a small corner shop told me that Ma's house was on a short street which started at a point in back of the store.

The house was a small, unpainted structure set far back on a barren, grassless plot. Ma's huddled figure could be seen on the front porch. As I approached, she greeted me pleasantly and invited me inside.

Studying the stooped little figure, I recalled the stories of witchcraft which the neighbors had told me and the association the old woman was rumored to have with spirits and magic charms and other sinister things. Her dark, thin face was criss-crossed with myriads of wrinkles. Eyes which were narrowed to mere slits gleamed occasionally with surprising brilliance. One side of her grizzled hair hung in a tangled mass, while the other side was neatly braided. Her short, stocky figure was garbed in a fitted dark red velveteen coat, beneath which showed the hem of a faded black dress and that of a green apron.

The house consisted of the one room which we now entered. There was so much crowded into the small space that it took awhile before the blurred, massed objects could be seen as separate items. With difficulty, I made my way to the rocking chair which Ma indicated, and looked around me. A square wooden table in the center of the room held a large assortment of miscellaneous articles. I studied these curiously, noticing in particular four glass jars which held what seemed to be literally hundreds of small orange and purple papers. Grouped about the room were a large number of chairs, most of them so close together that they bumped into one another. Larger pieces of furniture were a rusty iron stove, a couch draped with a faded red coverlet, and an old-fashioned marble-topped dressing table which was almost hidden by its burden of bottles, pitchers, glasses, handleless cups, and jars filled with crepe-paper flowers.

The walls were covered with a confusion of pictures. From all four sides, the image of Bishop Grace [a charismatic African American religious leader of the early twentieth century] looked down, elaborately attired in a flowing robe and towering head-dress. There were also two or three religious pictures, a collection of postcards, newspaper clippings, and several large framed photographs which Ma told me were of her various relations.

From one wall was suspended a wooden hat rack, and here reposed a number of men's hats. All of these were in a badly battered condition and ranged in style from a boy's cap to a tall evening hat which still bore unmistakable traces of grandeur.

Ma told me that she was 103 years old. She talked of the days of her youth when she had worked as a laundress. For years, she had served in this capacity in a series of small country hotels. However, as she grew older, the work proved too laborious for her failing strength, and she had been forced to depend on her children for support. During the past few years, her husband and the children one after another had died. The husband had died of old age, and the son and daughter had contracted what seemed at first like heavy colds but had subsequently developed into serious illnesses. Now, Ma was all alone in the world.

"I know just when de end was to come for each one of 'em," she said. "Something tell me each time. It is de same way wid me. I will know just when it's time for me to die. Just a short time back, I was so sick I couldn't raise my head. All de folks would come in an' look at me an' shake dey heads.

"I hear 'em whisper, 'She is sho sick. She never get up.' I laugh to myself. I knowed dey was wrong an' I wasn't ready to die. I don't let on I hear 'em. Some of 'em was so sho dat I was goin' to die dat dey move out my best furniture. I lay dere an' watch 'em move it out one piece after another. I was so sick I couldn't do nothin' to stop 'em. When I get better an' start to get around, dose folks sho was scared. Dey don't never come here no mo'. Guess dey is worried 'bout what I might do to 'em."

Ma paused momentarily, and glancing again about the crowded little room I wondered just where the stolen articles of furniture had been placed and whether or not the guilty persons' worries were concerned with the black magic that Ma might direct against them.

"I don't 'member just how I get to be a root doctor," the old woman continued. "Seems like ya just have to be born wid de knowledge. I just allus seemed to know how to work cures and make medicines. Folks was allus comin' to me an' asking me to cure some illness. When I was young an' went out washin', I didn't have much time to cure folks. Den when I get too old to work steady, I stay home an' mix up all kind of charms an' magic remedies. 'Fore I know it, mo' and mo' folks hear 'bout me, an' soon dey come from all over to be cured. I been workin' roots now for years.

"Folks used to dribe here in cars most any time, even in de middle of de night. I never knew when dey would be comin'. Some would have crazy spells an' spasms an' be ravin' mad. Someone had put a spell on 'em. I work over 'em, an' when dey leave dey would be all right again."

I tried to find out just how Ma effected these cures, but she was not yet ready to divulge her secrets. She stared blankly for a moment and didn't answer.

"Do you still cure people?" I asked.

"No, ma'am, not very much no mo'. Ya see, de police drag me into court some years back for practicin' witchcraft. Some of de neighbors complain. I show 'em right dere in de courtroom how I mix de medicine an' how I could help folks. Dey couldn't prove nothin', an' dey just let me go. After dat, I mighty careful, though.

"I tell ya just how witchcraft started," Ma continued. "In de beginnin', de devil was an angel in heaven. He tell a lie, an' dat start all de trouble in de world. He see how God make man, an' he say, 'I could make man, too.' God say, 'Ya make ya a man,' so Lucifer make a man an' show him to God. God say, 'Blow breath in ya man.' Lucifer, he blow breath in de nostrils, an' out of de nose come lizards an' snakes an' maggots an' spiders an' all such things. After dat, dese things was allus evil. When dey see what de debbil had done, dey drive him out of heaven. He fall hard, an' he land an' make hell. An' dis was de start of witchcraft an' evil in de world. An' long as dere be a debbil in hell, dere will be witchcraft in de world."

The subject of witchcraft reminded me of the many tales of witches related by the neighbors. In response to my question as to whether or not her slumbers were disturbed by the nocturnal visits of these creatures, Ma nodded her gray head sagely. She went on to tell me of some of her personal experiences with them.

"Dey is dead spirits what come an' ride ya when ya is asleep. Dey take different shapes—sometime dey is men, sometime dey is women, an' sometime animals. When ya wake up, dey is chokin' an' smotherin' ya. When dey sees ya is awake, dey jump off an' go away. In de mornin', ya is all worn out.

"Dere is all kind of spirits. Course, everybody can't see 'em. Only dose who is born wid a caul. Now, I was born wid a caul, an' I see 'em all de time. Lots of time, I is walkin' 'long de road an' dere is a spirit right next to me, talkin' just like a person.

"One night, a spirit come to me in my sleep an' tell me 'bout where a pot of gold was buried. It take me out of de house an' down de road to a clump of oak trees. Dere sho nuff was de rim of de pot. De next day, I take my husband to de place. We use a long stick called a strikin' rod. We dig down wid it, an' when it hit de pot we dig right down in dat spot. We find a big pot, an' it have a heap of money an' spoons an' knives in it. All of dis make me rich for a long time, an' I buy lots of things. I have some of de money an' de knives an' spoons right now someplace in de house.

"Unless a spirit show ya a pot of gold, ya can't dig it up. One time, my brother come to visit me, an' he see a big round thing like a rim of a pot in de ground. He get a strikin' rod an' start diggin'. De wind start to howl, an' all sorts of strange noises begin. De rod just go down in de ground, an' de pot sink deeper an' deeper. My brother get scared an' stop diggin'. He just have to give up tryin' to get dat pot."

Ma seemed by now to have overcome her reluctance to talk of her methods of curing people, and she went into detail to tell me just how she compounded certain remedies.

"I need a piece of homespun, a pot of fire, an' some Holy Oil," she said. "I anoint de head wid de oil an' wrap de head. I den rub de head an' say de words what work de cure. Den I unwrap de homespun an' throw it in de fire. I hit it nine licks an' punch it nine times. Den de fits just go 'way. Dragon's blood an' incense is good, too, to use in cures."

Conjures, Ma told me, were often made of ground-up snakes and lizards. If the enemy desired to put a spell on or to cripple the victim, he put this powder in his shoes, hat, or other articles of apparel. However, if the intention was to kill, the poison was put in whiskey or coffee and fed to the victim.

Conjures could be turned back on the enemy who designed them, if the intended victim manufactured a "Hell Fire Gun." To make this, it is necessary to have some old newspapers, some fire, a tub of old rags, gunpowder, sulphur, and an old turpentine bottle. Ma said she had made many of these guns, and that one time she had caught three enemies instead of one. Of course, most people would be ignorant of how to make such a gun and would have to consult a root doctor who had knowledge of such things.

"Many years back, dere was a woman who live right next door to me. She allus make out like she was my friend an' talk nice to my face, but she was really my enemy. She was jealous of what I had, an' she was plottin' how to do me evil.

"One mornin', I go over to her house, an' she sittin' down eatin' her breakfast. She say, 'Sit down an' have some coffee wid me.'

"I have de coffee, an' I stay an' talk. After a time, I come back home. All of a sudden, I feel sick—my head was dizzy an' I have to sit down on a chair. Right away, I knowed dat woman have kunjuh me. Dere was a charm in dat coffee. I goes right out in de yard an' I gets what I need to make a Hell Fire Gun. I have to work fast, for dat kunjuh was powerful strong, an' I was feelin' worse all de time.

"In just a little time, I have made de gun, an' I shoot it off. 'Stead of catchin' one enemy, I catch three. Dat woman have got two man to help her kunjuh me, an' when I shoot off de gun it get 'em all. First thing ya know, I hear how first one an' then another was sick. Dey get worse an' worse, an' after a time dey all die."

A cure for a conjured person was also described by the root worker. This consisted of rattlesnake root, a new cup, a quarter-pint of gin, and some sulphur. The root is first washed in the new cup and the gin and sulphur added. The mixture is stirred nine times one way, then nine times in the opposite direction, then punched nine times. It is now ready for consumption. Ma insisted that this remedy had never failed to cure, even when the victim had almost wasted away.

The ingredients for another concoction were dragon's blood, sugar, sulphur, and spice. All of this when well blended made an effective charm for warding off evil and assuring good luck. The powder should be sprinkled in the four corners of a room, going diagonally from one corner to the other, thus forming a cross. This powder is used for matters of the heart, for business, for luck in games—in short, for any emergency. "To make a love charm, de women put de powder in cologne an' put it on demselves. Dey is sure to catch de men dis way," the old woman explained.

Ma rummaged around on the shelves of the cupboard of the cabinet and brought forth several samples of her magic art. She displayed a yellow, waxy substance which she said was dragon's blood and many different powders. A brown paper package contained a charm which she said she had compounded for a client.

The queer-looking purple and orange papers in the glass jars on the table were magic charms which were used for a variety of purposes.

As I prepared to depart, Ma urged me to return and get some of her magic powders for protection against evil influences.

Shaking her gray head, upon which there now perched incongruously a saucy navy blue and red skating cap, she told me warningly, "Ya never can tell who is a witch an' who is workin' 'gainst ya. Folks can do ya lots of harm, an' ya have to be careful dat nobody don't put a spell on ya."

EMMALINE HEARD

Born: Unknown
Age: Unknown
Master: Unknown
Place: Henry County, Georgia
Interviewer: Minnie Ross
Source: First Series, Library of Congress Rare Book Room
    Collection, Georgia Narratives, volume 12A, page 32

Mrs. Emmaline Heard has proved to be a regular storehouse for conjure and ghost stories. Not only this but she is a firm believer in the practice of conjure. To back up her belief in conjure is her appearance. She is a dark-brown-skinned woman of medium height and always wears a dirty towel on her head. The towel, which was at one time white, gives her the weird look of an old-time fortune teller.

Tuesday, December 8, 1936, a visit was made to her home and the following information was secured:

"There was onct a house in McDonough, and it was owned by the Smiths that was slave owners way back yonder. Now, this is the truth 'cause it was told to me by old Uncle Joe Turner, and he 'sperience it. Nobody could live in this house, I don't care how they tried. Dey say this house was hainted and anybody that tried to stay there was pulled out of bed by a haint. Well, sir, they offered the house and a thousand dollars to anyone who could stay there overnight. Uncle Joe said he decided to try it, so sho nuff he got ready one night and went to this house to stay. After while, says he, something come in the room and started over to the bed, but 'fore it got there he said, 'What in the name of the Lord you want with me?' It said, 'Follow me. There is a pot of gold buried near the chimney. Go find it and you won't be worried with me no more.' De next morning, Uncle Joe went out there and begin to dig, and sho nuff he found the gold, and 'sides that he got the house. Dis here is the truth. Uncle Joe's house is right there in McDonough now, and anybody round there will tell you the same thing 'cause he was well known. Uncle Joe is dead now.

"Anudder story that happened during slavery time and was told to me by Father was this: The master had a old man on his plantation named Jimson. Well, Jimson's wife was sick and had been for nearly a year. One day there, she wanted some peas, black-eyed peas, but old man Harper didn't have none on his plantation, so Jimson planned to steal off that night and go to old Marse Daniel's farm, which was four miles from Marse Harper's farm, and steal a few peas for his wife. Well, between midnight and day, he got a sack and started off down the road. Long after while, a owl started hootin', *Sho-o-o are-e-e, who-o o-o*, just like someone saying, 'Who are you?' Jimson got scared, pulled off his cap, and run all the way to old man Daniel's farm. As he run, he was saying, 'Sir, dis is me, old Jimson,' over and over again. Now, when he got near the farm, old Daniel heard him and got up in the loft to watch him. Finally, old Jimson got dere and started creeping up in the loft. When he got up dere, chile, Marse Daniel grabbed his whip and 'most beat Jimson to death.

"This here story happened in Mississippi years ago, but the folks that tell it to me said it was the truth. There was a woman that was sick; her name was Mary Jones. Well, she lingered and lingered till she finally died. In them days, folks all around would come to the settin'-up if somebody was dead. They done sent some men after the casket. Since they had to go thirty miles, they was a good while getting back, so the folkses decided to sing. After while, they heard the men come up on the porch, and somebody got up to let 'em in. Chile, just as they opened the door, that woman set straight up on that bed, and such another runnin' and getting out of that house you never heard. But some folks realized she wasn't dead, so they got the casket out de way so she wouldn't see it, 'cause they was 'fraid she would pass out sho nuff. Just the same, they was 'fraid of her, too. The man went off and come back with pistols, guns, sticks, and everything, and when this woman saw 'em she said, 'Don't run, I won't bother you.' But chile, they left there in a big hurry, too. Well, this here Mary went to her sister's house and knocked on the door and said, 'Let me in. This is Mary. I want to talk to you and tell you where I've been.' The sister's husband opened the door and let her in. This woman told 'em that God had brought her to and that she had been in a trance with the Lord. After that, everyone was always afraid of that woman, and they wouldn't even sit next to her in the church. They say she is still living.

"This happened right yonder in McDonough years ago. A gal went to a party with her sweetheart, and her ma told her not to go. Well, she went on anyhow in a buggy. When they got to the railroad crossing, a train hit the buggy and killed the gal, but the boy didn't get hurted at all. Well, while they was settin' up with this dead gal, the boy comes 'long there in his buggy with another gal, and do you know that horse stopped right in front of that house and wouldn't budge one inch. No matter how hard he whip that horse, it wouldn't move. Instead, he reared and kicked and jumped about and almost turned the buggy over. The gal in the buggy fainted. Finally, a old slavery-time man come along and told him to get a quart of whiskey and pour it around the buggy and the haint would go away. So they done that, and the spirit let 'em pass. If a haint liked whiskey in they lifetime and you pour it round where they's at, they will go away."

The following are true conjure stories supposedly witnessed by Mrs. Heard:

"There was a Reverend Dennis that lived below the federal prison. Now, he was the preacher of the Hardshell Baptist church in this community. This man stayed sick about a year and kept gettin' different doctors, and none of them did him any good. Well, his wife kept on at him till he decided to go to see Dr. Geech. His complaint was that he felt something run up his legs to his thighs. Old Dr. Geech told him that he had snakes in his body, and they was put there by the lady he had been going wid. Dr. Geech give him some medicine to take and told him that on the seventh day from then that woman would come and take the medicine off the shelf and throw it away. Course, Reverend Dennis didn't believe a thing he said, so sho nuff she come just like Dr. Geech said and took the medicine away. Dr. Geech told him that he would die when the snakes got up in his arm, but if he would do like he told him he would get all right. Dis woman had put this stuff in some whiskey, and he drunk it, so the snakes breed in his body. After he quit taking the medicine, he got bad off and had to stay in the bed. Sho nuff, the morning he died, you could see the snake in his arm. The print of it was there when he died. The snake stretched out in his arm and died, too.

"I got a son named Jack Heard. Well, somebody fixed him. I was in Chicago when that happened, and my daughter kept writing to me to come home 'cause Jack was acting funny, and she thought maybe he was losing his mind. They was living in Thomasville then, and every day he would go sit round the store and laugh and talk, but just as soon as night would come and he would eat his supper them fits would come on him. He would squeal just like a pig, and he would get down on his knees and bark just like a dog. Well, I come home and went over to see a old conjure doctor. He says to me, 'That boy is hurt, and when you go home you look in the corner of the mattress and you will find it.' Sho nuff, I went home and looked in the corner of the mattress, and there the package was. It was a mixture of his hair and bluestone wrapped up in red flannel with new needles running all through it. When I went back, he says to me, 'Emmaline, have you got eight dimes?' 'No,' I said, 'but I got a dollar.' 'Well, get that dollar changed into ten dimes, and take eight of 'em and give 'em to me.' Then he took Jack in a room, took off his clothes, and started to rubbin' him down with medicine. All at the same time, he was saying a ceremony over him. Then he took them eight dimes, put 'em in a bag, and tied them around Jack's chest somewhere so that they would hang over his heart. 'Now, wear them always,' says he to Jack. Jack wore them dimes a long time, but he finally drunk 'em up anyway. That doctor cured him, 'cause he sho woulda died."

The following are a few facts as related by Mrs. Heard concerning an old conjure doctor known as Aunt Darkas.

"Aunt Darkas lived in McDonough, Georgia, until a few years ago. She died when she was 128 years old. But chile, lemme tell you, that woman knowed just what to do fer you. She was blind, but she could go to the woods and pick out any kind of root or herb she wanted. She always said the Lord told her what roots to get, and always 'fore sunup you would see her in the woods with a short-handled pick. She said she had to pick 'em 'fore sunup, I don't know why.

"If you was sick, all you had to do was go to see Aunt Darkas and tell her. She had a well, and after listening to your complaint she would go out there and draw a bucket of water and set it on the floor, and then she would wave her hand over it and say something. She called this 'healing the water.' After this, she would give you a drink of water. As she hand it to you, she would say, 'Now, drink, take this and drink.' Honey, I had some of that water myself, and believe me, it goes all over you and makes you feel so good. Old Aunt Darkas would give you a supply of water and tell you to come back fer more when that was gone. Old Aunt Darkas said the Lord gave her power and vision, and she used to fast for a week at a time. When she died, there was a piece in the paper 'bout her.

"This here is sho the trufe, and if you don't believe it go out to Southview Cemetery and see Sid Heard, my oldest son; he been out there over twenty years as sexton and bookkeeper. Yessir, he told it to me, and I believe it. This happen long ago, ten or fifteen years. There was a couple that lived in Macon, but their home was in Atlanta, and they had a lot out to Southview. Well, they had a young baby that took sick and died, so they had the baby's funeral there in Macon. Then they put the coffin in the box, placed the label on the box, then brought it to Atlanta. Folks are always buried so that they head faces the east. They say when Judgment Day come and Gabriel blow that trumpet, everybody will rise up facing the east. Well, as I was saying, they came here. Sid Heard met 'em out yonder and instructed his men for arrangements for the grave and everything. A few weeks later, the woman called Sid Heard up long distance. She said, 'Mr. Heard.' 'Yes, ma'am,' he said. 'I call you to tell you me and my husband can't rest at all.' 'Why?' he asked. 'Because we can hear our baby crying every night, and it is worrying us to death. Our neighbors next door say our baby must be buried wrong.' Sid Heard said, 'Well, I buried the baby according to the way you got the box labeled.' 'I am not blaming you, Mr. Heard, but if I pay you will you take my baby up?' 'Yes, ma'am, I will if you want me to. Just let me know the day you will be here, and I'll have everything ready.' 'All right,' said she.

" 'Well,' said Sid Heard, 'the day she was to come, she was sick and instead sent a carload of her friends.' The men got busy and started digging till they got to the box. Sho nuff, after they opened it, they found the baby had been buried wrong; the head was facing the west instead of the east. They turned the box around and covered it up. The folks then went on back to Macon. A week later, the women called up again. 'Mr. Heard,' she says. 'Yes, ma'am,' says he. 'Well, I haven't heard my baby cry at all in the past week. I wasn't there, but I know the exact date you took my baby up, 'cause I never heard it cry no more.'

"If you are eating with a mouthful of food and sneeze, that sho is a true sign of death. I know that 'cause years ago I was havin' breakfast with my son Wylie and one other boy, and Wylie sneezed and said, 'Mama, I'm so sorry. I just couldn't help it, the sneeze came on me so quick.' I just sat there and looked at him and began to wonder. Two weeks later, my brother rode up and announced my mother's death. That one sign that's true, yes, sir.

"If a picture falls off the wall, someone in the family will die.

"If you dream about teeth, if one falls out, that's another sign of death.

"Another sign of death just as sho as you live is to dream of a person naked. I dreamed my son was naked but his body was covered with hair. Three months later, he died. Yessir, that sho is a true sign.

"Just as sho as your left hand itches, you will receive money. If fire pops on you from the stove or fireplace, you will get a letter.

"If the left side of your nose itches, a man is coming to the house. If it itches on the tip, he will come riding.

"If the right side of your nose itches, a woman is coming to the house."

Following are stories told to Mrs. Heard by her parents, which took place during the period of slavery. They are supposed to be true, as they were experienced by the persons who told them.

"My mother told me a story that happened when she was a slave. When her mistress whipped her, she would run away to the woods, but at night she would sneak back to nurse her babies. The plantation was on old McDonough Road, so to get to the plantation she had to come by a cemetery, and you could see the white stones shining in the moonlight. This cemetery was near a cut in the road that people said was hainted, and they still say old McDonough Road is hainted. One night, Mama said she was on her way to the plantation walking on the middle of the road, and the moon was shining very bright. When she reached this cut, she heard a noise, *Clack! clack! clack!* and this noise reminded a person of a lot of machines moving. All at once, a big thing as large as a house came down the side of the road. She said it looked like a lot of chains, wheels, posts all mangled together, and it seemed that there were more wheels and chains than anything else. It kept on by making that noise, *Clack! clack! clack!* She stood right still till it passed and came on to the farm. On her way back, she say she didn't see it anymore, but right till today that spot is hainted. I have knowed horses to run away right there with people and hurt them. Then sometimes they have reared and kicked and turned to go in the other direction. You see, horses can see haints sometimes when folks can't. Now, the reason for this cut being hainted was because old Dave Copeland used to whip his slaves to death and bury them along there."

The next story was told to Mrs. Heard by her father, who experienced it as a slave boy.

"My father said when he was a boy, him and two more boys run away from the master 'cause the master whipped 'em. They set out and walked till it got dark, and they saw a big old empty house settin' back from de road. Now, this house was three or four miles from any other house. So they went in and made a fire and laid down 'cause they was tired from running from the pattyrollers. Soon, they heard something say, *Tap! tap! tap!* Down the stairs it came, a loud noise, and then, 'Oh, Lordy, Master, I ain't goin' do it no more. Let me off this time.' After a while, they heard this same noise like a house falling in and the same words: 'Oh, Lordy, Master, I ain't goin' do it no more. Let me off this time.' By this time, they had got good and scared, so my pa said he and his friends looked at each other and got up and ran away from that house just as fast as they could go. Nobody knowed why this old house was hainted, but they believed that some slaves had been killed in it."

The next is a story of the jack-o'-lantern, as told by Mrs. Heard.

"Old South River on the Jonesboro Road is just full of swampy land, and on rainy, drizzly nights jack-o'-lanterns will lead you. One night, my uncle started out to see his girl, and he had to go through the woods and the swamps. When he got in de swampland he had to cross a branch, and the night was dark and drizzly, so dark you could hardly see your hand before your face. Way up the creek, he saw a little bright light, so he followed it thinking he was on his way. All night long, he said he followed this light up and down the swamp but never got near to it. When day came, he was still in the creek and had not gone any distance at all. He went and told the folks, and they went back to the swamps and saw his tracks up and down in the mud. Later, a group of 'em set out to find the jack-o'-lantern, and way down the creek they found it on a bush. It looked like soot hanging down from a bush, burnt out. My uncle went to bed 'cause he was sleepy and tired down from walking all night."

The following two stories related by Mrs. Heard deal with practices of conjure. She definitely states that they are true stories, and backs up this statement by saying she is a firm believer in conjure.

"As I told you before, my daddy came from Virginia. He was bought there by old Harper and brought to McDonough as a slave boy. Well, as the speculator drove along south, he learned who the different slaves were. When he [Mrs. Heard's father] got here, he was told by the master to live with old Uncle Ned 'cause he was the only bachelor on the plantation. The master said to old Ned, 'Well, Ned. I have bought me a fine young plowboy. I want him to stay with you, and you treat him right.' Every night, Uncle Ned would make a pallet on the floor for Daddy and make him go to bed. When he got in bed, he [Uncle Ned] would watch him out of the corner of his eye, but Daddy would pretend he was asleep and watch old Uncle Ned to see what he was going to do. After a while, Uncle Ned would take a broom and sweep the fireplace clean, then he would get a basket and take out of it a whole lot of little bundles wrapped in white cloth. As he lay out a package, he would say, 'Grasshoppers,' 'Spiders,' 'Scorpion,' 'Snake heads,' etc., then he would take the tongs and turn 'em around before the blaze so that they would parch. Night after night, he would do this same thing until they had parched enough, then he would beat all of it together and make a powder; then put it up in little bags. My daddy was afraid to ask old Uncle Ned what he did with these bags but heard he conjured folks with 'em. In fact, he did conjure a gal 'cause she wouldn't pay him any attention. This gal was very young and preferred talking to the younger men, but Uncle Ned always tried to hang around her and help hoe, but she would always tell him to go do his own work 'cause she could do hers. One day, he said to her, 'All right, madam, I'll see you later. You won't notice me now, but you'll wish you had.' When the dinner came and they left the field, they left their hoes standing so they would know just where to start when they got back. When that gal went back to the field, the minute she touched that hoe she fell dead. Some folks say they saw Uncle Ned dressing that hoe with conjure.

"My sister Lizzie sho did get fixed, honey, and it took a old conjurer to get the spell off of her. It was like this: Sister Lizzie had a pretty peach tree, and one limb spreaded out over the walk, and just as soon as she would walk under this limb she would stay sick all the time. The funny part 'bout it was that while she was at other folks' house she would feel all right, but the minute she passed under this limb she would begin to feel bad. One day, she sent for a conjurer, and he looked under the house, and sho nuff he found it stuck in the sill. It looked like a bundle of rags, red flannel all stuck up with needles and everything else. This old conjurer told her that the tree had been dressed for her, and 'twould be best for her to cut it down. It was a pretty tree, and she sho did hate to cut it down, but she did like he told her.

"Yes, child, I don't know whether I've ever been conjured or not, but sometimes my head hurts and I wonder."

EASTER SUDIE CAMPBELL

Born: 1865
Age: Seventy-two
Master: Will Grooms
Place: Caldwell County, Kentucky
Interviewer: Mamie Hanberry
Source: First Series, Library of Congress Rare Book Room
   Collection, Kentucky Narratives, volume 16K, page 90

*Aunt Easter, as she is called, has followed the pro-
fession of a midwife for forty years. She is still active
and works at present among the Negroes of Hopkinsville.*

"Yes, sho, I make my own medicines, humph, dat ain't no
trouble. I cans cure scrofula wid burdock root and one-half spoon
of citrate of potash. Just make a tea of burdock root an' add the
citrate of potash to it. Sassafras is good for de stomach an' cleans
ya out good. I's uses yeller percoon root for de sore eyes.

"When I stayed wid Mrs. Porter, her chaps [young children]
would break out mighty bad wid sores in de fall of de year, and
I's told Mrs. Porter I's could cure dat, so I's got me some elder-
berries an' made pies out of it an' made her chaps eat it, an'
dey were soon cured.

"If it won't for de white folks, I sho would have a hard time. My man, he just went away, an' I ain't never seed him again, an' I's had five chilluns, an' de white folks have helped me all dese years. Dese trifling niggers, dey won't help dey own kind of folks.

"If you's got de toothache, I makes a poultice of scraped Irish potatoes an' puts it on de jaw on de side de tooth is aching, an' dat sho takes de fever out of de tooth. I's blows tobacco smoke in de ear, an' dat stops de earache.

"When I goes on a baby case, I just let nature have its way. I's always tease de baby. De first thing I does is to blow my breath in de baby's mouth, an' I spanks it just a little so it will cry, den I gives it warm catnip tea so if it is gwine to have de hives dey will break out on it. Some cases need one kind of tea an' some another. I give sinkfield [vine] tea for de colic. It is just good for young baby's stomach. I's been grannying for nigh on forty year, an' I's only lost two babies dat were born alive. One of dese were de white man's fault—dis baby were born wid de jaundice, an' I tolds dis white man to go to de store an' get me some calomel, an' he says, 'Whoever heard of givin' a baby such truck?' an' so dat baby died.

"Of course, you's can tell whether the baby is gwine to be a boy or girl 'fore 'tis born. If de mother carries dat child more on de left an' high up, dat baby will be a boy, an' if she carries it more to de middle dat will be a girl. Mothers oughta be more careful while carrying dere chilluns not to get scared of anything, for dey will sho mark dere babies wid terrible ugly things. I knows once a young woman were expecting, an' she goes blackberry hunting, an' a bull cow wid long horns got after her, an' she was so scairt dat she threw her hands over her head, an' when dat baby boy were born he had two nubs on his head just like horns beginning to grow, so I's had her call her doctor, an' dey cuts 'em off. One white woman I's waited on like hot chocolate, an' she always wanted more. She never had nuff of dat stuff. An' one day, she spills some on her leg, an' it just splashed an' burned her, an' when dat gal were born she had a big brown spot on her leg just like her mammy's scar from de burn. Now, you see, I knows ya can mark de babies.

"Dere were a colored woman once I's waited on dat had to help de white folks kill hogs, an' she never did like hog liver, but de white folks told her to take one home an' fix it for her supper. Well, she picked dat thing up an' started off wid it an' it made her feel creepy all over, an' dat night her baby were born, a gal child, an' de print of a big hog liver were standing out all over one side of her face. Dat side of her face is all blue or purplish an' just the shape of a liver. An' it's still dere.

"I's grannied over three hundred chilluns, an' I knows what I's talking about.

"Hee, hee, hee! One day, dere were a circus in Hopkinsville, an' a black woman I's were going to wait on were on de street to watch for de parade, an' wid de bands playing an' de wild varmints an' things dis woman give birth to dat girl chile on de corner of Webber and Seventh Street. Dat gal sho got a funny name—Es-pe-cu-liar.

I did not get the drift of the story, so I asked her what was so funny about the name. Of course, it is a name I had never heard before, so the following is what the girl's mother said about it to Aunt Easter.

"Well, the gal's mammy thought it were just peculiar dat dat happened when she were looking at the parade.

"Yah, yah! I sho remember how de ol' folks uster dress. De women wore hoop skirts, an' de men wore tight breeches.

De nightgowns had big long sleeves wid a cuff at de hand an' a deep hem at de bottom of de gown. Dese gowns were made of domestic, an' when dey were washed an' starched an' ironed dey were so stiff dey could stand alone. De men an' de women both wore nightcaps. If de gown were a dress-up gown, dey were homemade with crochet lace in de front an' lots an' lots of tucks. Some of 'em had deep ruffles on 'em at the bottom.

"When my pappy come home from de war—he were on de gov'ment side—he brung a pistol back wid him dat shot a ball. Dey had caps on it an' used dese in de war. De Ku Klux come after him one night, an' he got three of 'em wid dis pistol. Nobody ever knowed who got dose Kluxes.

"Sho dere is ghosts. One night as I were going home from work, de tallest man I ever seed followed me wid de prettiest white shirt on, an' then he passed me an' waited at de corner. I were feeling creepy an' want to run but just couldn't get my legs to move, an' when I's get to de corner where he were I said, 'Good evening,' an' I seed him plain as day, an' he did not speak an' just disappeared right 'fore my eyes.

"Den I went to de fishpond one day fishing an' catched two or three big fish. When I went home, I thought I'd go back dat night, an' I begun to dig some fishing worms, an' my boss, he saw me an' asked what I doing. I told him I were going to de pond to fish dat night. He said, 'Don't you go to dat pond tonight, Easter, for if you does something will run you away.' I just laughed at him, an' dat night I an' my boy, we goes to de pond, an' as we were standing in dere quiet-like, we heared something squeeching like a new saddle an' horses trotting. We listened an' waited, an' something went into dat pond right 'twixt us like a ball of fire. We sho did leave dere, an' de next morning my boss asked me if we catched anything, an' we told him what we saw, an' he said he knowed we would be run away, for he were run away himself.

"Course dere is hainted houses. Dese haints in dese places just won't leave you alone. When I's were living in Princeton, Uncle Lige, my mammy's brother, an' I's moved into a cabin one Christmas day an' were going to stay dere, an' dat night we were setting before de fire, an' de firelight were bright as day, when I looks up at de wall, for I hears a scratching noise, an' dere were a big white cat on de wall wid all his hair standing, an' dat cat just jumps from one wall to de other, an' Uncle Lige an' me just open dat cabin door an' started to de other cabins on de place, an' we seed dat thing dat were bigger dan any cat I ever seed just come through dat door in de air an' hit de front gate. Dis gate had a iron weight on it so it would stay shut, an' dis thing hit at de top, then went away. I never seed where it went. Dis gate just banged an' banged all night. We could hear from de other cabin. Uncle Lige an' me moved away next day, an' other people moved in dis cabin, an' dey saw de same thing, an' nobody would stay dere. Den sometime after dis, de cabin were torn down.

"Once, I had a dream. I knowed I near 'bout saw it. I always did cook every night a pot of beans on de fire for de chilluns to eat next day while I was at work, an' Lizzie my daughter uster get up in de night an' get her some beans an' eat 'em, an' dis dream were so real dat I couldn't tell if it were Lizzie or not, but dis woman just glided by my bed an' went 'fore de fire an' stood dere, den she just went 'twixt my bed an' went by de wall. I just knowed when I woke up dat my child was sick dat lived away from home, an' wanted my son to take me to see her. He said he would go himself, an' so he went, an' when he come back he had a headache, an' 'fore morning dat nigger were dead. So, you see, dat were de sign of de dream. I were just warned in de dream an' didn't have sense nuff to know it."

Josephine Anderson

Born: Unknown
Age: Unknown
Master: Unknown
Place: Baker County, Florida
Interviewer: Jules Frost
Source: First Series, Library of Congress Rare Book Room
Collection, Florida Narratives, volume 17A, page 1

"I cain't tell nothin' 'bout slavery times 'cept what I heared folks talk about. I was too young to remember much, but I recollect seein' my gramma milk de cows an' do de washin'. Grampa was old, an' dey let him do light work, mostly fish an' hunt.

"I don't 'member nothin' 'bout my daddy. He died when I was a baby. My stepfather was Stephen Anderson, an' my mammy's name was Dorcas. He come from Virginny, but my mammy was borned an' raised in Wilmington. My name was Josephine Anderson 'fore I married Willie Jones. I had two half-brothers younger'n me, John Henry an' Ed, an' a half-sister, Elsie. De boys had to mind de calves an' sheeps, an' Elsie nursed de missus' baby. I done de cookin' mostly, an' helped my mammy spin.

"I was only five year old when dey brung me to Sanderson, in Baker County, Florida. My stepfather went to work for a turpentine man, makin' barrels, an' he work at dat job till he drop dead in de camp. I reckon he musta had heart disease.

"I don't recollect ever seein' my mammy wear shoes. Even in de winter, she go barefoot, an' I reckon cold didn't hurt her feet no more'n her hands an' face. We all wore dresses made o' homespun. De thread was spun an' de cloth wove right in our own home. My mammy an' granmammy an' me done it in spare time.

"My weddin' dress was blue—blue for true. I thought it was de prettiest dress I ever see. We was married in de courthouse, an' dat be a mighty happy day for me. Mo' folks dem days got married by layin' a broom on de floor an' jumpin' over it. Dat seals de marriage an' at de same time brings 'em good luck.

"Ya see, brooms keeps haints away. When mean folks dies, de old debbil sometimes don't want 'em down dere in de bad place, so he makes witches out of 'em an' sends 'em back. One thing 'bout witches, dey gotta count everything 'fore dey can get across it. You put a broom across your door at night, an' old witch's gotta count every straw in dat broom 'fore she can come in.

"Some folks can just nachly see haints better'n others. Teeny, my gal, can. I reckon dat's 'cause she been borned wid a veil—you know, a caul, somethin' what be over some babies' faces when dey is borned. Folks borned wid a caul can see spirits an' tell what's gonna happen 'fore it comes true.

"Use to worry Teeny right smart, seein' spirits day an' night. My husband say he gonna cure her, so he taken a grain o' corn an' put it in a bottle in Teeny's bedroom overnight. Then he planted it in de yard an' drive plenty sticks round de place. When it was growin' good, he put leaf mold round de stalk an' watch it every day, an' tell us don't *nobody* touch de stalk. It raise three big ears o' corn, an' when dey was good roastin' size he pick 'em off an' cook 'em an' tell Teeny eat every grain offen all three cobs. He watch her while she done it, an' she ain't never been worried wid haints no more. She sees 'em just the same, but dey don't bother her none.

"Fust time I ever knowed a haint to come into our quarters was when I was just big nuff to go out to parties. De game what we use to play was spin de plate. Every time I think on dat game, it gives me de shivers. One time, there was a strange young man come to a party where I was. Said he name Richard Green, an' he been takin' care o' horses for a rich man what was gonna buy a plantation in dat county. He look kinda slick an' dressed-up—different from de rest. All de gals begin to cast sheep's eyes at him, an' hope he gonna choose 'em when dey start playin' games.

"Pretty soon, dey begin to play spin de plate, an' it come my turn fust thing. I spin it an' call out, 'Mr. Green!' He jumps to de middle o' de ring to grab de plate, an' *bang*, 'bout four guns go off all at once, an' Mr. Green fall to de floor plum dead, shot through de head.

" 'Fore we knowed who done it, de sheriff an' some more men jump down from de loft, where dey been hidin', an' tell us quit hollerin' an' don't be scairt. Dis man be a bad desper . . . you know, one o' them outlaws what kills folks. He some kinda foreigner, an' just tryin' make believe he a niggah so's they don't find him.

"Well, we didn't feel like playin' no more games, an' forever after dat you couldn't get no niggahs to pass dat house alone after dark. Dey say de place was hainted, an' if you look through de winder any dark night you could see a man in dere spinnin' de plate.

"I sho didn't never look in, 'cause I done seen more haints already dan I ever wants to see again. One night, I was goin' to my grandy's house. It was just comin' dark, an' when I got to de creek an' start across on de foot log, dere on de other end o' dat log was a man wid his haid cut off an' layin' plum over on his shoulder. He look at me kinda pitiful an' don't say a word, but I closely never waited to see what he gonna talk about. I pure flew back home. I was so scairt I couldn't tell de folks what done happened till I set down an' got my breath.

" 'Nother time not so long ago, when I live down in Gary, I be walkin' down de railroad track soon in de mornin', an' 'fore I knowed it dere was a white man walkin' 'long side o' me. I just thought it were somebody, but I wasn't sho, so I turn off at de fust street to get 'way from dere. De next mornin', I be goin' to work at de same time. It were kinda foggy an' dark, so I never seen nobody till I mighty nigh run into dis same man, an' dere he goes, 'bout half a step ahead o' me, his two hands restin' on his behind.

"I was so close up to him I could see him plain as I see you. He had fingernails dat long, all cleaned an' polished. He was tall an' had on a derby hat an' stylish black clothes. When I walk slow, he slow down, an' when I stop he stop, never once lookin' round. My feets make a noise on de cinders 'tween de rails, but he don't make a mite o' noise. Dat was de fust thing got me scairt, but I figger I better find out for sho iffen he be a spirit, so I say, good an' loud, 'Looky here, mister, I just an old colored woman, an' I know my place, an' I wish you wouldn't walk wid me, counta what folks might say.'

"He never looked round no more, as if I wasn't there. I cut my eyes round to see if there is somebody I can holler to for help. When I looked back, he was gone—gone, like dat, without makin' a sound. Den I knowed he be a haint, an' de next day when I tell somebody 'bout it dey say he be de gemmen what got killed at de crossin' a spell back, an' other folks has seen him just like I did. Dey say dey can hear babies cryin' at de trestle right near dere, an' ain't nobody yet ever found 'em.

"Dat ain't de only haint I ever seen. One day, I go out to de smokehouse to get a meal o' taters. It was after sundown but still purty light. When I gets dere, de door be unlocked an' a big man standin' half inside. 'What you doin' stealin' our taters?' I hollers at him, an' *pow!* He gone, just like dat. Did I get back to dat house! We mighty glad to eat grits an' cornbread dat night.

"When we livin' at Titusville, I see my old mammy comin' up de road just as plain as day. I stand on de porch, fixin' to run an' meet her, when all of a sudden she be gone. I begin to cry an' tell de folks I ain't gonna see my mammy again. An' sho nuff, I never did. She die at Sanderson, back in north Florida, 'fore I got to see her.

"Does I believe in witches? S-a-a-y, I knows more 'bout 'em dan to just believe. I been *rid* by one. Right here in de house. You ain't never been rid by a witch? Well, you mighty lucky. Dey come in de night, ginnerly soon after you drop off to sleep. Dey put a bridle on your head an' a bit in your mouth an' a saddle on your back. Den dey take off their skin an' hang it up on de wall. Den dey get on you, an' some nights dey like to ride you to death. You try to holler but you cain't, counta the iron bit in your mouth, an' you feel like somebody holdin' you down. Den dey ride you back home an' into your bed. When you hit de bed, you jump an' grab de covers, an' de witch be gone, like dat. But you know you been rid mighty hard 'cause you all wet wid sweat an' you feel plum tired out.

"Some folks say you just been dreamin', counta de blood stop circulating in your back. Shucks! Dey ain't never been rid by a witch, or dey stop sayin' dat.

"Old witch doctor, he want ten dollars for a piece o' string what he say some kinda charm words over. Tells me to make a image o' dat old witch wid dough an' tie dat string round its neck, then when I bake it in de oven it swell up an' de magic string shut off her breath. I didn't have no ten dollar, so he say iffen I get up five dollar he make me a hand—you know, what colored folks calls a jack. Dat be a charm what will keep de witches away. I knows how to make one, but dey don't do no good without de magic words, an' I don't know 'em. You take a little pinch o' dried snakeskin an' some graveyard dirt an' some red pepper an' a lock o' your hair wrapped round some black rooster feathers. Den you spit whiskey on 'em an' wrap 'em in red flannel an' sew it into a boll 'bout dat big. Den you hang it under your right armpit, an' every week you give it a drink o' whiskey to keep it strong an powerful. Dat keep de witches from ridin' you.

"But nary one o' dese charms work wid dis old witch. I got a purty good idea who she is, an' she got a charm powerfuller dan both of 'em. But she cain't get across flaxseed, not till she count every seed. You don't believe dat? Huh! I reckon I knows—I done tried it out. I gets me a li'l bag o' pure fresh flaxseed an' I sprinkle it all round de bed. Then I put some on top of de mattress an' under de sheet. Den I goes to bed an' sleeps like a baby, an' dat old witch don't bother me no more.

"Only once. Soon's I wake up, I light me a lamp an' look on de floor, an' dere side o' my bed was my dress, layin' right over dat flaxseed, so's she could walk over on de dress, big as life. I snatch up de broom an' throw it on de bed, den I go to sleep. An' I ain't *never* been bothered no more.

"Some folks reads de Bible backwards to keep witches from ridin' em, but dat don't do me no good 'cause I cain't read. But flaxseed work so good I don't be studyin' night-ridin' witches no more."

AMANDA STYLES

Born: 1857
Age: Eighty
Master: Jack Lambert
Place: Unknown
Interviewer: Whitley
Source: First Series, Library of Congress Rare Book Room
    Collection, Georgia Narratives, volume 13A, page 343

On November 18, 1936, Amanda Styles, ex-slave, was interviewed at her residence. Styles is about eighty years of age and could give but a few facts concerning her life as a slave. Her family belonged to an ordinary class of people neither rich nor poor. Her master, Jack Lambert, owned a small plantation and one other slave besides her family, which included her mother, father, and one sister. The only event during slavery that impressed itself on Mrs. Styles was the fact that when the Yanks came to their farm they carried off her mother, and she was never heard of again.

Concerning superstitions, signs, and other stories pertaining to this, Mrs. Styles related the following signs and events. As far as possible, the stores are given in her exact words.

"During my day, some folks could read the signs by looking in the clouds. A woman that whistled was marked to be a bad woman. If a black cat crossed your path, you sho would turn round and go anudder way. It was bad luck to sit on a bed, and when I was small I was never allowed to sit on the bed."

Following are stories related by Mrs. Styles which had their origin during slavery and immediately following slavery.

"During slavery time, there was a family that had a daughter, and she married, and everybody said she was a witch 'cause at night dey said she would turn her skin inside out and go round riding folks' horses. De next morning, de horses' manes would be tied up. Now, her husband didn't know she was a witch, so somebody tole him he could tell by cutting off one of her limbs, so one night the wife changed to a cat, and the husband cut off her forefinger what had a ring on it. After that, de wife would keep her hand hid 'cause her finger was cut off, and she knowed her husband would find out that she was the witch.

"My mother said her young mistress was a witch, and she, too, married, but her husband didn't know that she was a witch, and she would go round at night riding horses and turning the cows' milk into blood. De folks didn't know what to do— instead of milk, they had blood. So one day, a old lady come there and told 'em that a witch had been riding the cow, and to cast off the spell they had to take a horseshoe and put it in the bottom of the churn, and then the blood would turn back to milk and butter. Sho nuff, they did it and got milk.

"Anudder man had a wife that was accused of being a witch, so he cut her leg off and it was a cat's leg, and when his wife came back her leg was missing.

"They say there was a lot of conjuring, too, and I have heard 'bout a lot of it. My husband told me he went to see a woman once dat had scorpions in her body. The conjurer did it by putting the blood of a scorpion in her body, and this would breed more scorpions in her. They had to get anudder conjurer to undo the spell.

"There was anudder family that lived near and that had a daughter, and when she died they say she had a snake in her body.

"My husband said he was conjured when he was a boy and had to walk with his arms outstretched—he couldn't put 'em down at all and couldn't even move 'em. One day, he met a old man, and he said, 'Son, what's de matter wid you?' 'I don't know,' he said. 'Then why don't you put your arms down?' 'I can't.' So the old man took a bottle out of his pocket and rubbed his arms straight down till they got all right.

"He told me, too, 'bout a woman fixing her husband. This woman saw anudder man she wanted, so she had her husband fixed so he would throw his arms up, get on his knees, and bark just like a dog. So they got some old man that was a conjurer to come and cure him. He woulda died if they hadn't got that spell off him.

"My father told me that a woman fixed anudder one 'cause she married her sweetheart. She told her he never would do her any good, and sho nuff she fixed her so dat she would have a spell every time she went to church. One day, they sent for her husband and asked him what was the matter with her, and he told them that this other woman had fixed her with conjure. They sent for a conjurer, and he came and rubbed some medicine on her body, and she got all right.

"During slavery time, the master promised to whip a nigger, and when he came out to whip him instead he just told him, 'Go on, nigger, 'bout your business.' De nigger had fixed him by spitting as far as he could spit, so the master couldn't come any nearer than that spit.

"I know a nigger that they said was kin to the devil. He told me that he could go out 'hind the house and make some noise and the devil would come and dance with him. He said the devil learned him to play a banjo, and if you wanted to do anything the devil could do, go to a crossroad, walk backwards, and curse God. But don't never let the devil touch any of your works or anything that belonged to you or you would lose your power.

"The nearest I ever came to believing in conjure was when my stepmother got sick. She fell out with a woman that lived with her daughter 'cause this woman had did something to her daughter, and so she called her a black kinky-head hussy, and this woman got fightin' mad and said to her, 'Never mind, you'll be nappy and kinky-headed, too, when I get through wid you.' My ma's head turned real white and funny right round the edge, and her mind got bad, and she used to chew tobacco and spit in her hands and rub it in her head, and very soon all her hair fell out. She even quit my father after living with him twenty years, saying he had poisoned her. She stayed sick a long time, and de doctors never could understand her sickness. She died, and I will always believe she was fixed."

After she related the last story, my interview with Mrs. Styles came to an end. I thanked her and left, wondering over the strange stories she had told me.

Mother/Child

"A custom prevailed about the Southern states that the firstborn of each slave should be the son or daughter of her master, and the girls were forced into maternity at puberty. The mothers naturally resisted this terrible practice, and Harriett was determined to prevent her child being victimized. . . . One night, the mother received directions through a dream in which her escape was planned. She told the child about the dream and instructed her to carry out orders that they might escape together."

Adah Isabelle Suggs interview

LuLu Wilson
Reproduced from the collection of the Library of Congress,
LC-USZ62-125326
(interview on pages 146-51)

Mother/Child

In the summer of 2005, an American opera by the name of *Margaret Garner* was first performed onstage by the Michigan Opera Theatre; the opera was composed by Richard Danielpour, and the libretto was written by Toni Morrison. The opera tells the story of Margaret Garner, a fugitive slave from Kentucky who, when surrounded by pursuing federal marshals in Cincinnati, slits her daughter's throat and attempts to kill her other children with a shovel. The Garners had attempted the highly unusual act of fleeing slavery as a family after years of sexual abuse and the imminent threat of Margaret's daughter being sold away from her. At Margaret's fugitive-slave trial, antislavery activist Lucy Stone spoke of the horror that would put a slave mother at her daughter's throat: "The faded faces of the Negro children tell too plainly to what degradation the female slaves submit. Rather than give her daughter to that life, she killed it. If in her deep maternal love she felt the impulse to send her child back to God, to save it from coming woe, who shall say she had no right not to do so? That desire had its root in the deepest and holiest feelings of our nature—implanted in black and white alike by our common father."[39]

The story of Margaret Garner is immortalized in Toni Morrison's novel *Beloved*, whose character Sethe is inspired by the trials and tribulations that Margaret faced in attempting to raise her children within the context of an unholy institution. The theme of a mother's love for her children is pervasive in *Beloved*. Sethe's love for her daughter, and even the ghost of her daughter, is such that she is plagued by the challenges she faces as an enslaved mother: "Sethe [who had abandoned her child to flee slavery] pleaded for forgiveness, counting, listing again and again her reasons: that Beloved was more important, meant more to her than her own life. That she would trade places any day. Give up her life, every minute and hour of it, to take back just one of Beloved's tears. Did she know it hurt her when mosquitoes bit her baby? That to leave her on the ground to run into the big house drove her crazy? That before leaving Sweet Home Beloved slept every night on her chest or curled on her back?"[40]

In reality, Sethe's psychological confrontation with the ghost of her daughter is the recapitulation of her own struggle with her mother, who was hanged after fleeing the plantation, leaving Sethe behind. Thus, the multigenerational conflict between mother and child depicted in *Beloved* is actually a theme taken directly from the lives of enslaved mothers.

If the commercial use of enslaved mothers as "breeders" to enrich the household of the plantation owners rendered women and children commodities, the process was somewhat redeemed by the sacred role of motherhood within the West African cosmos. In that world view, women provided the continuity by which the community survived and, in matrilineal societies, the manner in which wealth and power were passed from one generation to another. Childbirth was a hallowed responsibility, and the birth of a child was a sacred rite of passage signifying transition from childhood to adulthood and the establishment of status within family and tribal life. The connection with one's mother was the most important relationship in the psychological and social world of the child and, as such, formed the basis of the child's interaction with all other elements in the environment.[41]

In both West African society and the enslaved community, women were the link of kinship in worlds where war, hunting, and labor made men absent and brought them in close contact with death. Fathers were often distant both psychologically and physically, a separation that provided all the more impetus for developing intense relationships with mothers. Women often raised their children in the absence of, or with only sporadic contact with, the fathers; time and again within the ex-slave narratives are stories of fathers coming on weekends and holidays and having to return to their home plantations to reassume their responsibilities. Unfortunately, the legacy of this problem persists into the modern era, as the majority of African American children live in homes without fathers, though the proportion living in two-parent families has risen significantly since 1995.[42]

Slave women's ability to have children was vital to their status within the community and the plantation. Child bearers were greatly valued as a commodity; nonproductive women were sent to the field or were sold. At the same time, this created a difficult challenge for women as they came of childbearing age. On the one hand, they were pressured to have children. On the other hand, their allure attracted men of the planter community and was therefore a great threat to their well-being. The conflicts were many and the resolutions few, but as Deborah Gray White notes in *Ar'n't I a Woman*, "living on the precipice of destruction as the slave did, giving birth was a life affirming action. It was, ironically, an act of defiance."[43]

Giving birth may have been liberating in the life of slave women and may have provided them some degree of safety, but it also posed a challenge to their freedom. Enslaved women who had children were unlikely to run away and leave their sons and daughters behind, and if they ran away with their children, they would be all the more easily captured and returned. The punishment for such an action might well be the selling of the very children the mothers had tried to protect. Thus, the story of the capture of Margaret Garner and her family is all the more a curiosity, as very few women fled with their children. As Harriet Jacobs explains in the narrative of her enslavement, becoming a fugitive and leaving one's children was a source of great discord: "But now that I was certain my children were to be put in their power, in order to give them a stronger hold on me, I resolved to leave them that night. . . . I shut all the windows, locked all the doors, and went up to the third story, to wait till midnight. How long those hours seemed, and how fervently I prayed that God would not forsake me in this hour of utmost need! I was about to risk every thing on the throw of a die; and if I failed, O what would become of me and my poor children? They would be made to suffer for my fault."[44]

And yet some did escape with their children! In this section, Adah Isabelle Suggs's narrative tells of another mother from Kentucky who made her escape with her daughter across the Ohio River, but into Indiana instead of Ohio. It was not an easy trip. The first time they attempted it, they were captured and the mother was imprisoned in an upper room where she could only talk to her daughter through the window. However, Adah's mother was determined to prevent her daughter from being victimized. It seems that there were greater forces involved in this process as well; one night, the mother received directions for the escape in a dream. Lauana Creel, the WPA interviewer, tells most of this story in the third person, as she does in many of her interviews, but it is still an interesting story. In her inimitable style, Ms. Creel asks, "What greater hope can be given to the mortal than the hope cherished by Adah Isabelle Suggs?"

Lulu Wilson, also from Kentucky, was taken to Texas before the Civil War. She was the daughter of a free Creek Indian whose mother lived on a small homestead with only two slaves. When her father failed to bring forth children, her mother's owner "set the nigger hounds on my paw," who fled to the free territory. Her mother was then forced to take up with a "young buck," and the children proceeded to come; her owner would wait until Lulu's mother was in the field and then sell her children to the highest bidder. Lulu describes what would happen next: "When she'd come back, she'd raise a ruckus. Then many the time I seed her plop right down to a settin' and cry 'bout it. But she 'lowed they weren't nothin' could be done, 'cause it's the slavery law." Lulu was able to stay with her mother until she was thirteen, when her owner "married me outen the Bible to a nigger 'longin' to a nephew of his'n." Eventually, freedom came and the "slavery law" was ended for Lulu Wilson.

From the Indiana ex-slave narratives comes the story of an enslaved woman from Kentucky who was never overworked and generally had enough to eat but remembers many slaves who, according to her interviewer, "were not as fortunate as they were." One slave mother was considered more profitable without her infant than with it, so the situation was taken care of; the result "preyed on her mind to such an extent she developed epilepsy." Such stories of cruelty inflicted upon slaves "would make your hair stand on ends."

The last narrative in the section also comes from Kentucky via Indiana. Ethel Daugherty was a mixed-blood Indian with blue eyes whose great-grandmother was from Kentucky. She tells of the lives of slaves and "the great wrong that had been done" to her race. In addition, she tells of the great wrong done to her.

ADAH ISABELLE SUGGS

Born: 1852
Age: Eighty-five
Master: Jackson McClain
Place: Henderson County, Kentucky
Interviewer: Lauana Creel
Source: First Series, Library of Congress Rare Book Room
    Collection, Indiana Narratives, volume 06B, page 189

Among the interesting stories connected with former slaves, one of the most outstanding ones is the life story of Adah Isabelle Suggs. Indeed, her escape from slavery, planned and executed by her anxious mother, Harriett McClain, bears the earmarks of fiction, but the truth of all related occurrences has been established by the aged Negro woman and her daughter Mrs. Harriett Holloway, both citizens of Evansville, Indiana.

Born in slavery before January the twenty-second, 1852, the child Adah McClain was the property of Colonel Jackson McClain and Louisa, his wife.

According to the customary practice of raising slave children, Adah was left at the Negro quarters of the McClain plantation, a large estate located in Henderson County three and one-half miles from the village of Henderson, Kentucky. There, she was cared for by her mother. She retains many impressions gained in early childhood of the slave quarters; she remembers the slaves singing and dancing together after the day of toil. Their voices were strong, and their songs were sweet. "Master was good to his slaves and never beat them" were her words concerning her master.

When Adah was not yet five years of age, the mistress, Louisa McClain, made a trip to the slave quarters to review conditions of the Negroes. It was there she discovered that one little girl had been developing ideas and ideals; the mother had taught the little one to knit tiny stockings, using wheat straws for knitting needles.

Mrs. McClain at once took charge of the child, taking her from her mother's care and establishing her room at the residence of the McClain family.

Today, the aged Negro woman recalls the words of praise and encouragement accorded her accomplishments, for the child was apt, active, responsive to influence, and soon learned to fetch any needed volume from the library shelves of the McClain home.

She was contented and happy, but the mother knew that much unhappiness was in store for her young daughter if she remained as she was situated.

A custom prevailed about the Southern states that the first-born of each slave should be the son or daughter of her master, and the girls were forced into maternity at puberty. The mothers naturally resisted this terrible practice, and Harriett was determined to prevent her child being victimized.

One planned escape was thwarted; when the girl was about twelve years of age, the mother tried to take her to a place of safety, but they were overtaken on the road to the ferry, where they hoped to be put across the Ohio River. They were carried back to the plantation, and the mother was mildly punished and imprisoned in an upstairs room.

The little girl knew her mother was imprisoned and often climbed up to a window where the two could talk together.

One night, the mother received directions through a dream in which her escape was planned. She told the child about the dream and instructed her to carry out orders that they might escape together.

The girl brought a large knife from Mrs. McClain's pantry, and by the aid of that tool the lock was pried from the prison door, and the mother made her way into the open world about midnight.

A large tobacco barn became her refuge, where she waited for her child. The girl had some trouble making her escape; she had become a useful and necessary member of her mistress's household, and her services were hourly in demand. The daughter, young mistress Annie McClain, was afflicted from birth, having a cleft palate and later developing heart dropsy, which made regular surgery imperative. The Negro girl had learned to care for the young white woman and could draw the bandages for the surgeon when the young mistress underwent surgical treatment.

The child loved her young mistress, and the young mistress desired the good slave should be always near her, so patient waiting was required by the Negro mother before her daughter finally reached their rendezvous.

Under cover of night, the two fugitives traveled the three miles to Henderson, where they secreted themselves under the house of Mrs. Margaret Bentley until darkness fell over the world to cover their retreat. Imagine the frightened Negroes stealthily creeping through the woods in constant fear of being recaptured. Federal soldiers put them across the river at Henderson, and from that point they cautiously advanced toward Evansville. The husband of Harriett, Lilton McClain, and her son Jerome were volunteers in a Negro regiment. The operation of the Federal statute providing for the enlistment of slaves made enlisted

Negroes free, as well as their wives and children, so by that statute Harriett McClain and her daughter should have been given their freedom.

When the refugees arrived in Evansville, they were befriended by free Negroes of the area. Harriett obtained a position as maid with the Parvine family. "Miss Hallie and Miss Genevieve Pervine were real good folks," declares the aged Negro Adah when repeating her story. After working for the Misses Pervine for about two years, the Negro mother had saved enough money to place her child in "pay school," where she learned rapidly.

Adah McClain was married to Thomas Suggs January 18, 1872. Thomas was a slave of Bill McClain, and it is believed he adopted the name Suggs because a Mr. Suggs had befriended him in time of trouble. Of this fact neither the wife nor daughter have positive proof. The father has departed this life, but Adah Suggs lives on with her memories.

Varied experiences have attended her way. Wifehood and devotion, motherhood and care she has known, for she has given fifteen children to the world. Among them were one set of twins—daughters—and triplets—two sons and a daughter. She is a beloved mother to those of her children who remain near her and says she is happy in her belief in God and Christ and hopes for a glorious hereafter where she can serve the Lord Jesus Christ and praise Him eternally.

What greater hope can be given to the mortal than the hope cherished by Adah Isabelle Suggs?

LULU WILSON

Born: 1839
Age: Ninety-seven
Master: Wash Hodges
Place: Barren County, Kentucky
Interviewer: Heloise Foreman
Source: Second Supplemental Series, Texas Narratives,
    volume 10T, page 4191

Lulu Wilson, blind, bedridden Negro, does not know her age but believes that she is ninety-seven. She was born near the Mammoth Cave in Kentucky. Lulu owns a little home at 1108 Good Street, Dallas, Texas.

"Course I's born in slavery, ageable as I am. I'm a old-time slavery woman, and the way I been through the hackles, I got plenty to say 'bout slavery. Lulu Wilson says she knows they ain't no good in it, and they better not bring it back.

"My paw weren't no slave. He was a free man 'cause his mammy was a full-blood Creek Indian. But my maw was born in slavery, down on Wash Hodges' paw's place, and he give her to

Wash when he married. That was the only woman slave what he had, and one man slave, a young buck. My maw say she took with my paw and I's born, but a long time passed and didn't no more younguns come, so they say my paw am too old and wore-out for breedin' and wants her to take with this here young buck. So the Hodges set the nigger hounds on my paw and run him away from the place, and Maw allus say he went to the free state. So she took with my step-paw, and they must of pleased the white folks what wanted niggers to breed like livestock, 'cause she birthed nineteen chillun.

"When I's li'l, I used to play in that big cave they calls Mammoth, and I's so used to that cave it didn't seem like nothin' to me. But I was real li'l then, for soon as they could they put me to spinnin' cloth. I 'members plain, when I was li'l, there was talk of war in them parts, and they put me to spinnin', and I heared 'em say it was for sojers. They marched round in a li'l, small drove and practices shootin'.

"Now, when I was li'l, they was the hardest times. They'd nearly beat us to death. They taken me from my mammy, out the li'l house built onto they house, and I had to sleep in a bed by Missus Hodges. I cried for my maw, but I had to work and wash and iron and clean and milk cows when I was 'most too li'l to do it.

"The Hodges had three chilluns, and the olderest one they was mean to, 'cause she so thickheaded. She couldn't learn nothin' out a book but was kinder and more friendly-like than the rest of the lot. Wash Hodges was just mean, poor trash, and he was a bad actor and a bad manager. He never could make any money, and he starved it outen the niggers. For years, all I could get was one li'l slice of sowbelly and a puny li'l piece of bread and a tater. I never had nuff to stave the hungriness outen my belly.

"My maw was cookin' in the house, and she was a link—— that am the best of its kind. She weren't 'fraid. Wash Hodges tried to whup her with a cowhide, and she'd knock him down and bloody him up. Then he'd go down to some his neighbor kin and try to get them to come help him whup her. But they'd say, 'I don't want to go up there and let Chloe Ann beat me up.' I heared Wash tell his wife they said that.

"When maw was in a tantrum, my step-paw wouldn't partialize with her. But she was a religious woman and believed time was comin' when niggers wouldn't be slaves. She told me to pray for it. She seed a old man what the nigger dogs chased and et the legs near off him. She said she was chased by them bloody hounds, and she just picked up a club and laid they skull open. She say they hired her out and sold her twice but allus brung her back to Wash Hodges.

"Now, Missus Hodges studied 'bout meanness more'n Wash done. She was mean to anybody she could lay her hands to, but special mean to me. She beat me and used to tie my hands and make me lay flat on the floor and she put snuff in my eyes. I ain't lyin' 'fore God when I say I knows that's why I went blind. I did see white folks sometimes what spoke right friendly and kindly to me.

"I gets to thinkin' now how Wash Hodges sold off Maw's chillun. He'd sell 'em and have the folks come for 'em when my maw was in the fields. When she'd come back, she'd raise a ruckus. Then many the time I seed her plop right down to a settin' and cry 'bout it. But she 'lowed they weren't nothin' could be done, 'cause it's the slavery law. She said, 'O, Lawd, let me see the end of it 'fore I die, and I'll quit my cussin' and fightin' and rarin'.' My maw say she's part Indian, and that 'countable for her ways.

"One day, they trucked us all down in a covered wagon and started out with the family and my maw and step-paw and five of us chillun. I know I's past twelve year old. We come a long way and passed through a free state. Some places, we drove for miles in the woods 'stead of the big road, and when we come to folks they hid us down in the bed of the wagon. We passed through a li'l place, and my maw say to look, and I seed a man gwine up some steps totin' a bucket of water. She say, 'Lulu, that man's your paw.' I ain't never think she's as considerable [considerate] of my step-paw as of my paw, and she give me to think as much. My step-paw never did like me, but he was a fool for his own younguns, 'cause at the end of the wars when they set the niggers free he tramped over half the country gatherin' up them younguns they done sold 'way.

"We went to a place called Wakefield, in Texas, and settled for some short passin' of time. They was a Baptist church next our house, and they let me go twice. I was fancified with the singin' and preachin'. Then we goes on to Chatfield Point, and Wash Hodges built a log house and covered it with weatherboarding and built my maw and paw quarters to live in. They turned to raisin' corn and taters and hawgs. I had to work like a dog. I hoed and milked ten cows a day.

"Missus told me I had ought to marry. She said if I'd marry she'd get me up in a white dress and give me a weddin' supper. She made the dress, and Wash Hodges married me outen the Bible to a nigger 'longin' to a nephew of his'n. I was 'bout thirteen or fourteen. I know it weren't long after that when Missus Hodges got a doctor to me. The doctor told me lessen I had a baby, old as I was and married, I'd start in on spasms. So it weren't long till I had a baby.

"In 'twixt that time, Wash Hodges starts layin' out in the woods and swamps all the time. I heared he was hidin' out from the war and was 'sposed to go 'cause he done been a volunteer in the first war, and they didn't have no luck in Kentucky.

"One night when we was all asleep, some folks whooped and woke us up. Two sojers come in, and they left more outside. They found Wash Hodges and said it was midnight and to get 'em something to eat. They et, and some more come in and et. They tied Wash's hands and made me hold a lamp in the door for them to see by. They had some more men in the wagon, with they hands tied. They drove away, and in a minute I heared the reports of the guns three or four times. Next day, I heared they was sojers and done shot some conscripts in the bottoms back of our place.

"Wash Hodges was gone away four years, and Missus Hodges was meaner'n the devil all the time. Seems like she just hated us worser than ever. She said blabber-mouth niggers done cause a war.

"Well, now, things just kind of drifts along for a spell, and then Wash Hodges come back and he said, 'Well, now, we done whup the hell out them blue bellies, and that'll learn 'em a lesson to leave us alone.'

"Then my step-paw seed some Federal sojers. I seed them, too. They drifted by in droves of fifty and a hundred. My step-paw 'lowed as how the Feds done told him they ain't no more slavery, and he tried to point it out to Wash Hodges. Wash says that's a new ruling, and it am that growed-up niggers is free, but chillun has to stay with they masters till they's of age.

"My maw was in her cabin with a week-old baby, and one night twelve Ku Kluxes done come to the place. They come in by ones, and she whupped 'em one at a time.

"I don't never recall just like, the passin' of time. I know I had my little-boy youngun, and he growed up, but right after he was born I left the Hodges and felt like it's good riddance. My boy died, but he left me a grandson. He growed up and went 'nother way, and they done somethin' to him, and he ain't got but one lung. He ain't peart [lively] no more. He's got four chillun, and he makes fifty dollars a month. I'm crazy 'bout that boy, and he comes to see me, but he can't help me none in a money way. So I'm right grateful to the president for gettin' my li'l pension. I done study it out in my mind for three years, and [I would] tell him, Lulu says if he will see they ain't no more slavery, and if they'll pay folks liveable wages, they'll be less stealin' and slummin' and goin's-on. I worked so hard. For more'n fifty years, I waited as a nurse on sick folks. I been through the hackles if any mortal soul has, but it seems like the president thinks right kindly of me, and I want him to know Lulu Wilson thinks right kindly of him.

PARTHENA ROLLINS

Born: 1853
Age: Eighty-four
Master: Ed Duvalle
Place: Scott County, Kentucky
Interviewer: Anna Pritchett
Source: First Series, Library of Congress Rare Book Room
     Collection, Indiana Narratives, volume 06B, page 167

Mrs. Parthena Rollins was born in Scott County, Kentucky, in 1853, a slave of Ed Duvalle, who was always very kind to all of his slaves, never whipping any of the adults but often whipped the children to correct them, never beating them. They all had to work but never overwork, and always had plenty to eat.

She remembers so many slaves who were not as fortunate as they were.

Once when the "nigger traders" came through, there was a girl, the mother of a young baby. The traders wanted the girl but would not buy her because she had the child. Her owner took her away, took the baby from her, and beat it to death right before the mother's eyes, then brought the girl back to the sale without the baby, and she was bought immediately.

Her new master was so pleased to get such a strong girl who could work so well and so fast.

The thoughts of the cruel way of putting her baby to death preyed on her mind to such an extent she developed epilepsy. This angered her new master, and he sent her back to her old master and forced him to refund the money he had paid for her.

Another slave had displeased his master for some reason. He was taken to the barn and killed, and was buried right in the barn. No one knew of this until they were set free, as the slaves who knew about it were afraid to tell, for fear of the same fate befalling them.

Parthena also remembers slaves being beaten until their backs were blistered. The overseers would then open the blisters and sprinkle salt and pepper in the open blisters, so their backs would smart and hurt all the more.

Many times, slaves would be beaten to death, thrown into sink-holes, and left for the buzzards to swarm and feast on their bodies.

So many of the slaves she knew were half fed and half clothed and treated so cruelly that it "would make your hair stand on ends."

Mrs. Rollins is in poor health, all broken up with " 'ritis."

She lives with a daughter and grandson, and said she could hardly talk of the happenings of the early days because of the awful things her folks had to go through.

ETHEL DAUGHERTY

Born: Unknown
Age: Unknown
Master: Unknown
Place: Unknown
Interviewer: Grace Monroe
Source: First Supplemental Series, Indiana Narratives,
    volume 05S, page 62

The experiences this family had while in slavery were very pitiful. Mrs. Daugherty told me the following incidents as she had heard them from her ancestors.

Her great-grandmother was a slave in Kentucky and was kept in the house to help with the cooking. The food she received was very good, but to those who were forced to work in the fields the treatment was terrible. They were lined up to wooden troughs, which were filled by pouring all the food in at once in the manner of slopping pigs.

This poor woman had four children sold, leaving her only one son, her youngest. All traces were lost permanently, due partly she thought because as soon as a child was bought it took the name of the owner, and after a few sales there was no way of identifying those lost. Many were shipped to different sections of the country and were not told who their parents were.

One incident was told of a mother and son (name not known) who were separated for years. The boy grew up and began keeping company with his mother. This man had a small scar almost invisible but happened to mention it, when his mother realized who he was and told him the particulars.

Mrs. Daugherty said there were a great many marriages in her race of kin before the Civil War closed. She said many of the well-built girls were taken by the master into his house and kept similar to Mormonism. She blamed this sin of mixed races on slavery but also thought there was still too much of racial intermarriages today, which she could only attribute to lack of self-control or the "devil turned loose."

At a slave sale, the wenches were forced to stand half-dressed for hours while a crowd of rough, drinking men bargained for them, examining their teeth, heads, hands, etc., at frequent intervals to determine their endurance. At other times, the owner of a nearby plantation might purchase a bunch of children privately, if he happened to desire them. If the slaves attempted to return to their parents, they were usually severely beaten and a closer watch kept over them the next time.

Mrs. Daugherty's first husband was a Grady. When people would remark that the name sounded Irish, they would be informed that the name had been in the family for generations— in fact, since slave days.

This lady was very sensible and realized the great wrong that had been done to her race. She herself is very sensitive over the fact that her eyes are blue. Her philosophy, however, is sound— that, through no fault of hers, she is not a full-blood. I have heard her advise her children to "stick to their color always." Her maiden name was Taylor. She said there are many Taylors found yet in Kentucky—all, as she said, "descendants of the white family who bestowed their name on the colored children years ago."

Her stepfather was a mixture of the white, Negro, and Indian races, his mother being an Indian squaw. When angry, he thought he was all Indian.

A fact was given to which they were very sensitive. Mr. Grady's grandmother was forced to live with her master. As a result of this union, his mother had very long hair. This was the first time Mrs. Daugherty said she had ever told anyone this, as the older Mrs. Grady always felt very badly about her origin.

At the close of the war, her ancestors were simply turned out to shift for themselves with no help from their old master. Many of them came to Indiana, but Mrs. Daugherty is the only one to locate in Jefferson County.

Herstory

"While he was eatin' it and takin' de last swallow of de apple, he was 'minded of de disobedience and choked twice. Ever since then, a man have a Adam's apple to 'mind him of de sin of disobedience. 'Twasn't long befo' de Lord come a-lookin' for them. Adam got so scared his face turned white right then, and next mornin' he was a white man wid long hair, but worse off than when he was a nigger."

Charity Moore interview

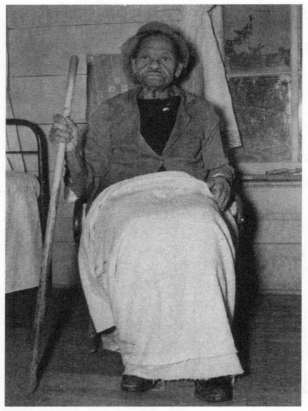

Mary Reynolds, ca. 1936-1938
Library of Congress, Manuscript Division
(interview on pages 176-186)

Herstory

"There has always existed a minority of women, like a minority of black Americans and American Indians, who did not sit still, who did not accept society's strictures upon them," writes June Sochen in *Herstory: A Woman's View of American History*. "These people deserve a place in the history books, as do the ordinary undistinguished souls in each period: their everyday life and ideas, their attitudes toward child-raising, their favorite novels and movies. All human actions, admittedly, are not of equal worth; all human thought is not of equal validity. Evaluations and distinctions must be made in historical, as well as all other kinds of writing. But the student and general reader of history should be aware of both elite and popular ideas, and become acquainted with the lot of so-called common people."[45]

The history of slavery in the United States has largely been told through the eyes of men and with the stories of men; it isn't that women have been totally ignored but that the understanding of the American experience of slavery has been shaped through the narratives of men. The most famous of all the slave narratives are the recollections of men. Frederick Douglass's *Narrative of the Life of Frederick Douglass, An American Slave, Written by Himself,* William Wells Brown's *Narrative of William W. Brown, A Fugitive Slave,* and Solomon Northup's *Twelve Years a Slave* were widely read during the nineteenth century and continue to dominate the landscape of the American slave narrative even unto the modern era. As such, these great works have provided the story of slavery.

Historians following in the footsteps of these authors focused their scholarship within the framework of the male experience of slavery; even the pictorial representations that we have are those of male slaves beaten and chained. What Deborah Gray White refers to as the "source problem" is evident in how the story of American slavery is told: "It is very difficult, if not impossible, to be precise about the effect of any single variable on female slaves. . . . Slave women were everywhere, yet they were nowhere."[46] Characteristic of the scholarship focusing on males as the quintessential representation of slavery is Stanley Elkins's controversial image of the slave as the "perpetual child," a stereotype mythologized by the caricature of Sambo. Though much has changed since Elkins's early-1960s work, the language used to describe slavery has changed little. "The leading characteristic of recent work, however, has been the belated recognition of the slave as a person," writes Peter Parish in *Slavery: The Many Faces of a Southern Institution.* "It is partly in reaction against Elkins and other interpretations of the slave as victim or object that a number of recent historians—Eugene Genovese, Herbert Gutman, Lawrence Levine, John Blassingame and others—have portrayed the slave as an active participant in the development of *his* own life style, and have sought to present a slave's eye view of slavery [italics added]. . . . Slavery was a system of many systems, with numerous exceptions to every rule.

There were urban slaves, industrial slaves, and hired slaves, and there were a quarter of a million free blacks in the South who lived constantly in the shadow of slavery. Slaves were domestic servants, craftsmen and artisans, overseers and drivers, as well as field hands."[47]

In the 1980s, things began to change slightly. Authors began to recontextualize the story of slavery to not just reflect the complicated landscape of the institution but to reframe discussions around how that landscape was portrayed. Even with an emerging body of women's literature looking at gender issues within the slave community, there is still, according to Jennifer Morgan, a "paucity of works that are organized around the lives of enslaved women"; there are currently only six historical monographs concerned primarily with enslaved women, and only three of these are based in the continental United States.[48] Following on the heels of Deborah Gray White's *Ar'n't I a Woman: Female Slaves in the Plantation South*, other more recent works such as Stephanie Camp's *Closer to Freedom: Enslaved Women and Everyday Resistance in the Plantation South* and Jennifer Morgan's *Laboring Women: Reproduction and Gender in New World Slavery* are opening the canon of scholarly works on the enslaved community to more nuanced and detailed explorations. Camp's work looks at the way that enslaved women rebelled against their entrapment by carving out their own personal space, a "rival geography," in which they refused to accept the power of those who held them in bondage. Morgan's project is more ambitious; she seeks to establish "a foundational methodology"[49] in writing early American history that demonstrates the impact of women on the development of slavery and proves that the presence of black women mattered. Her further purpose is "to open up the possibilities of interpretation," rather than to serve as the definitive word on the subject.[50]

It is toward that same end that this current project is dedicated. Therefore, this last section, entitled "Herstory," seeks solely to present some of the most interesting women's stories from the WPA ex-slave narratives. There is no common theme. The stories run from the Carolinas to the West; they were selected solely on the basis of their being intriguing and providing unique glimpses into the lives of the women of the era. If the history and the historiography of slavery have been dominated by a gender paradigm, then these stories are a brief attempt to undermine that ideology and tell history from the underside. If enslaved women had to endure prejudice based on the complicated dynamics of both race and gender, then their stories are twice removed from the body of history. This effort to lift up these ignored stories is so that we may examine a disjointed history and its dysfunctional interpretation. This section is presented with neither introductions nor any attempt at interpretation; the narratives are allowed to speak for themselves across history and to stand alone as chronicles of the experience of these women as agents of history.

There is a specific intent in placing this section at the end of a work subtitled *Personal Accounts of Women in Slavery*. These stories are meant to serve as a bridge to further investigation and interpretation. This project is meant as a starting point for the next generation of researchers and storytellers and as a means to allow them the opportunity to engage in a re-vision of history so as to come to terms with that part that lies untold. I trust that they can do much more than I could ever expect to. I offer them this gift in the hope that these women's lives will live on in future generations.

CHARITY MOORE

Born: 1862
Age: Seventy-five
Master: Brice
Place: Fairfield County, South Carolina
Interviewer: W. W. Dixon
Source: First Series, Library of Congress Rare Book Room
    Collection, South Carolina Narratives, volume 03A,
    page 205

One-quarter of a mile north of Woodward station and one hundred yards east of U.S. 21 is the beautiful residence of Mr. T. W. Brice. In the backyard is a two-room frame house. In this house lives Charity Moore and another aged Negro woman, said to be an octogenarian. They occupy the house together and exist on the goodness and charity of Mr. Brice. Charity was born a slave of Mr. Brice's father and has lived all her days in his immediate family.

"Don't you 'member my pa, Isaiah Moore? Course you does! He was de Uncle Remus of all de white chillun round dese parts. He sho was! I seen him a-settin' wid you, Marse Johnnie, Marse Boyco, and Dickie Brice in de backyard many a time. You-all was askin' him questions 'bout de tale he was a-tellin', and him shakin' his sides a-laughin'. He telled all them tales 'bout de fox and de rabbit, de squirrel, Brer Terrapin, and such like, long befo' they come out in a book. He sho did!

"My ma was name Nancy—dat was Pa's wedded wife. Dere was no bigamous nor concubine business goin' on wid us. My brothers was Dave, Solomon, Fortune, Charlie, and Brice. My sisters was Haley, Fannie, Sarah, Frances, Mary, and Margaret. Hold your writin' dere a minute. Dere was thirteen. Oh, yes, I left out Teets. Dat rounds them up—a baker's dozen, Marse Thomas use to 'low.

"My pa had Bible tales he never told de white chillun. Did you know dat my pa know de catechism from cover to cover, and from de back to de startin' end? Concord Church gived him a Bible for answering every question in the catechism. Here 'tis. [She produces a catechism published and dated 1840.] My pa maybe never telled you any Bible tales he told de colored chillun. He 'low dat de fust man, Adam, was a black man. Eve was ginger-cake color, wid long black hair down to her ankles. Dat Adam had just one worriment in de Garden, and dat was his kinky hair. Eve hate to see him sad, 'cause her love her husband as all wives ought to do, if they don't.

"Well, Adam play wid Eve's hair, run his fingers through it and sigh. Eve couldn't do dat wid his kinky hair. De debbil set up in de plum bushes and took notice of de trouble goin' on. Every day, Eve's hair growed longer and longer. Adam get sadder and sadder. De debbil in de plum bushes get gladder and gladder. Dere come a day dat Adam 'scused hisself from promenadin' in 'mong de flower beds wid his arms round Eve, a-holding up her hair. De debbil took de shape of a serpent, glided after Eve, and stole up and twisted hisself up into dat hair far enough to whisper in one of them pretty ears, 'Somebody's got something for to tell you dat will make Adam glad and like hisself again!

Keep your ears open all day long.' Then de serpent distangled hisself, dropped to de ground, and skedaddled to de red apple tree, close by de fountain. He knowed dat Eve was gwine dere to bathe. He beat her dere, 'cause she was walkin' sorta slow, grievin' 'bout Adam and thinkin' 'bout how to cheer him up.

"When she got dere, de old debbil done changed from a snake to a angel of light—a male angel, I reckon. He took off his silk beaver hat, flourished his gold-headed cane, and 'low, 'Good mornin'! Lovely day! What a beautiful apple, just in your reach too, ahem!' Eve say, 'I's not been introduced.' 'Well,' said de debbil, 'my subjects call me Prince, 'cause I's de Prince of Light. My given name is Lucifer. I's at your service, dear lady.' Eve 'flected, 'A prince—he'll be a king someday.' Then de debbil say, 'Of course, one of your beauty will one day be a queen. I seen a sadness on your lovely face as you come 'long. What might be your worry?' Eve told him, and he 'low, 'Just get Adam to eat one bite out dat apple 'bove your head, and in a night his hair will grow as long, be as black, and as straight as yourn.' She 'low, 'Us ain't 'lowed to eat of de fruit of de tree in de midst of de garden. Us dare not tech it, lest us die.' Then Satan stepped a distance dis way, then another way, and come back and say, 'Gracious lady! De tree not in de midst of de garden. De one in de midst is dat crab apple tree over yonder. Of course de good Lord didn't want you to eat crab apples.'

"De debbil done got her all mixed up. De apple looked so good, she reached up, and quick as you can say Jack Robinson she bite de apple and run to Adam wid de rest of it and say, 'Husband, eat quick and your hair will be as long, as black, and straight as mine in de mornin'.' While he was eatin' it and takin' de last swallow of de apple, he was 'minded of de disobedience and choked twice. Ever since then, a man have a Adam's apple to 'mind him of de sin of disobedience.

"'Twasn't long befo' de Lord come a-lookin' for them. Adam got so scared his face turned white right then, and next mornin' he was a white man wid long hair, but worse off than when he was a nigger. Dere was more to dat tale, but I disremember it now.

"I's livin' wid my young marster, Thomas, now. He took good care of my pa when he got so old and feeble he couldn't work no more. God'll bless Marse Tommie for all his goodness. When Pa Isaiah come to die, Marse Tommie come every day. One day in de evenin', he said in his gruff, kind way, 'Is dere anything I can do for you, Uncle Isaiah?' Pa say, 'Take care of Charity.' 'I will,' say Marse Tommie. Then he 'low, 'Ain't dere something else?' 'Yes,' Pa 'low, 'I want a white stone over de head of my grave.' 'What must I put on de stone?' asked Marse Tommie. 'Just my name and age,' said Pa. 'Oh, yes, dere ought to be something else,' says Marse Tommie. Pa shook his head. 'I want something else on it, Uncle Isaiah,' said Marse Tommie. Wid a tear and a smile, he raised his white head and said, 'You can put down, below de name and age, just dis: *As good as ever fluttered*.' And dat stone at Concord Cemetery 'tract more 'tention that any stone and epitaph in dat churchyard. Why, de white folks puts flowers on it sometimes.

"I wonder sometime in de winter nights, as de north wind blows 'bout de cracks in de house, if Pa is in Abraham's bosom. But I knows Pa; he's humble. There's so many white folks in dat bosom he'll just be content to lie in Isaac's bosom or maybe de prophet Isaiah's, for who he was named.

"Wait, dere! You have bad luck to leave by dat door. You comed in by de door, and you just leave by de same door. Some folks say nothin' to dat, but I don't want you to risk dat. Glad you come. Good-bye."

MARY ANNGADY

Born: 1857
Age: Eighty
Master: Franklin Davis
Place: Orange County, North Carolina
Interviewer: Pat Matthews
Source: First Series, Library of Congress Rare Book
    Room Collection, North Carolina Narratives,
    volume 4A, page 32

"I was eighteen years old in 1875, but I wanted to get married, so I gave my age as nineteen. I wish I could recall some of the ol' days when I was with my missus in Orange County, playing with my brothers and other slave children.

"I was owned by Mr. Franklin Davis, and my madam was Mrs. Bettie Davis. I and my brother used to scratch her feet and rub them for her; you know how old folks like to have their feet rubbed. My brother and I used to scrap over who should scratch and rub her feet. She would laugh and tell us not to do that way, that she loved us both. Sometimes, she let me sleep at her feet at night. She was plenty good to all of the slaves. Her daughter Sallie taught me my ABCs in Webster's *Blue Back* spelling book. When I learned to spell b-a-k-e-r, baker, I thought that was something. The next word I felt proud to spell was s-h-a-d-y, shady, the next l-a-d-y, lady. I would spell them out loud as I picked up chips in the yard to build a fire with. My missus Bettie gave me a *Blue Back* spelling book.

"My father was named James Mason, and he belonged to James Mason of Chapel Hill. Mother and I and my four brothers belonged to the same man, and we also lived in the town. I never lived on a farm or plantation in my life. I know nothing about farming. All my people are dead, and I cannot locate any of Marster's family if they are living. Marster's family consisted of two boys and two girls—Willie, Frank, Lucy, and Sallie. Marster was a merchant, selling general merchandise. I remember eating a lot of brown sugar and candy at his store.

"My mother was a cook. They allowed us a lot of privileges, and it was just one large, happy family with plenty to eat and wear, good sleeping places, and nothing to worry about. They were of the Presbyterian faith, and we slaves attended Sunday school and services at their church. There were about twelve slaves on the lot. The houses for slaves were built just a little ways back from Marster's house on the same lot. The Negro and white children played together, and there was little if any difference made in the treatment given a slave child and a white child. I have religious books they gave me. Besides the books they taught me, they drilled me in etiquette of the times and also in courtesy and respect to my superiors until it became a habit and it was perfectly natural for me to be polite.

"The first I knew of the Yankees was when I was out in my marster's yard picking up chips and they came along, took my little brother, and put him on a horse's back and carried him uptown. I ran and told my mother about it. They rode Brother over the town awhile, having fun out of him, then they brought him back. Brother said he had a good ride and was pleased with the Bluejackets, as the Yankee soldiers were called.

"We had all the silver and valuables hid, and the Yankees did not find them, but they went into Marster's store and took what they wanted. They gave my father a box of hardtack and a lot of meat. Father was a Christian, and he quoted one of the Commandments when they gave him things they had stolen from others. 'Thou shalt not steal,' quoth he, and he said he did not appreciate having stolen goods given to him.

"I traveled with the white folks in both sections of the country, North and South, after the War Between the States. I kept traveling with them and also continued my education. They taught me to recite, and I made money by reciting on many of the trips. Since the surrender, I have traveled in the North for various charitable Negro societies and institutions, and people seemed very much interested in the recitation I recited called 'When Malinda Sings.'

"The first school I attended was after the war closed. The school was located in Chapel Hill, North Carolina, and was taught by a Yankee white woman from Philadelphia. We remained in Chapel Hill only a few years after the war ended, when we all moved to Raleigh, and I have made it my home ever since. I got the major part of my education in Raleigh under Dr. M. H. Tupper, who taught in the Second Baptist Church, located on Blount Street. Miss Mary Lathrop, a colored teacher from Philadelphia, was an assistant teacher in Dr. Tupper's school. I went from there to Shaw Collegiate Institute, which is now Shaw University.

"I married Aaron Stallings of Warrenton, North Carolina, while at Shaw. He died, and I married Reverend Matthews Anngady of Monrovia, west coast of Africa, Liberia, pastor of First Church.

I helped him in his work here, kept studying the works of different authors and lecturing and reciting. My husband the Reverend Matthews Anngady died, and I gave a lot of my time to the cause of charity. While on a lecture tour of Massachusetts in the interest of this feature of colored welfare for Richmond, Virginia, the most colorful incident of my eventful life happened when I met Quango Hennadonah Perceriah, an Abyssinian prince, who was traveling and lecturing on the customs of his country and the habits of its people. Our mutual interests caused our friendship to ripen fast, and when the time of parting came, when each of us had finished our work in Massachusetts, he going back to his home in New York City and I returning to Richmond, he asked me to correspond with him. I promised to do so, and our friendship after a year's correspondence became love, and he proposed, and I accepted him. We were married in Raleigh by Reverend J. J. Worlds, pastor of the First Baptist Church, Colored.

"P. T. Barnum had captured my husband when he was a boy and brought him to America from Abyssinia, educated him, and then sent him back to his native country. He would not stay, and soon he was in America again. He was of the Catholic faith in America, and they conferred the honor of priesthood upon him, but after he married me this priesthood was taken away, and he joined the Episcopal Church. After we were married, we decided to go on an extensive lecture tour. He had been a headsman in his own country and a prince. We took the customs of his people and his experiences as the subject of our lectures. I could sing, play the guitar, violin, and piano, but I did not know his native language. He began to teach me, and soon I could sing the song 'How Firm a Foundation' in his language, which went this ways:

Ngama i-bata, Njami buyek
Wema Wemeta, Negana i bukek diol, di Njami,
i-diol de Kak
Annimix, Annimix hanci
Bata ba Satana i-bu butets
Bata ba Npjami i bunanan
Bata be satana ba laba i wa
Bata ba Njami ba laba Munonga

"We traveled and lectured in both sections—the North and the South—and our life, while we had to work hard, was one of happiness and contentment. I traveled and lectured as the Princess Quango Hennadonah Perceriah, wife of the Abyssinian prince. I often recited the recitation written by the colored poet Paul Lawrence Dunbar, 'When Malinda Sings,' to the delight of our audiences.

"The following incidents of African life were related to me by my husband Quango Hennadonah Perceriah, and they were also given in his lectures on African customs while touring the United States.

"The religion of the Bakuba tribe of Abyssinia was almost wholly pagan, as the natives believed fully in witchcraft, sorcery, myths, and superstitions. The witch doctor held absolute sway over the members of the tribe, and when his reputation as a giver of rain, bountiful crops, or success in the chase was at stake the tribes were called together, and those accused by the witch doctor of being responsible for these conditions through witchery were condemned and speedily executed.

"The people were called together by the beating of drums. The witch doctor, dressed in the most hellish garb imaginable, with his body painted and poisonous-snake-bone necklaces dangling from his neck and the claws of ferocious beasts—lions, leopards, and the teeth of vicious man-eating crocodiles—finishing up his adornment, sat in the middle of a court surrounded by the members of the tribe. In his hand, he carried a gourd which contained beads, shot, or small stones. He began his incantations by rattling the contents of the gourd, shouting and making many weird wails and peculiar contortions. After this had gone on for some time until he was near exhaustion, his face assumed the expression of one in great pain, and this was the beginning of the end for some poor, ignorant savage. He squirmed and turned in different directions with his eyes fixed with a set stare, as if in expectancy, when suddenly his gaze would be fixed on some member of the tribe and his finger pointed directly at him. The victim was at once seized and bound, the doctor's gaze never leaving him until this was done. If one victim appeased his nervous fervor, the trial was over, but if his wrought-up feelings desired more his screechings continued until a second victim was secured. He had these men put to death to justify himself in the eyes of the natives of his tribe for his failing to bring rain, bountiful crops, and success to the tribe.

"The witch doctor who sat as judge seemed to have perfect control over the savages' minds, and no one questioned his decisions. The persons were reconciled to their fate and were led away to execution while they moaned and bade their friends good-bye in the doleful savage style. Sometimes, they were put on a boat, taken out into the middle of a river, and there cut to pieces with blades of grass, their limbs being dismembered first and thrown into the river to the crocodiles. A drink containing an opiate was generally given the victim to deaden the pain, but often this formality was dispensed with. The victims were often cut to pieces at the place of trial with knives and their limbs thrown out to the vultures that almost continuously hover round the huts and kraals of the savage tribes of Africa.

"In some instances, condemned persons were burned at the stake. This form of execution is meted out at some of the religious dances or festivities to some of their pagan gods to atone and drive away the evil spirits that have caused pestilences to come upon the people. The victims at these times are tortured in truly savage fashion, being burned to death by degrees while the other members of the tribe dance around and go wild with religious fervor, calling to their gods while the victim screeches with pain in his slowly approaching death throes. Young girls, women, boys, and men are often accused of witchcraft. One method they used of telling whether the victim accused was innocent or guilty was to give them a liquid poison made from the juice of several poisonous plants. If they could drink it and live, they were innocent. If they died, they were guilty. In most cases, death was almost instantaneous. Some vomited the poison from their stomachs and lived.

"The Bakubas sometimes resorted to cannibalism, and my husband told me of a Bakuba girl who ate her own mother. Once, a snake bit a man, and he at once called the witch doctor. The snake was a poisonous one, and the man bitten was in great pain. The witch doctor whooped and went through several chants, but the man got worse instead of better. The witch doctor then told the man that his wife made the snake bite him by witchery, and that she should die for the act. The natives gathered at once in response to the witch doctor's call, and the woman was executed at once. The man bitten by the snake finally died, but the witch doctor had shifted the responsibility of his failure to help the man to his wife, who had been beheaded. The witch doctor had justified himself, and the incident was closed.

"The tribe ruled by a king has two or more absolute rules. The king's word is law, and he has the power to condemn any subject to death at any time without trial. If he becomes angry or offended with any of his wives, a nod and a word to his bodyguard and the woman is led away to execution. Any person of the tribe is subject to the king's will with the exception of the witch doctor.

"Executions of a different nature than the ones described above are common occurrences. For general crimes, the culprit, after being condemned to death, is placed in a chair shaped very much like the electric chairs used in American prisons in taking the lives of the condemned. He is then tied firmly to the chair with thongs. A pole made of a green sapling is firmly implanted in the earth nearby. A thong is placed around the neck of the victim under the chin. The sapling is then bent over and the other end of the thong tied to the end of the sapling pole. The pole stretches the neck to its full length and holds the head erect. Drums are sometimes beaten to drown the cries of those who are to be killed. The executioner, who is called a headsman, then walks forward, approaching the chair from the rear. When he reaches it, he steps to the side of the victim and with a large, sharp, long-bladed knife lops off the head of the criminal. The bodies of men executed in this manner are buried in shallow holes dug about two feet deep to receive their bodies.

"The rank and file of the savage tribes believe explicitly in the supernatural powers of the witch doctor, and his decisions are not questioned. Not even the king of the tribe raises a voice against him. The witch doctor is crafty enough not to condemn any of the king's household or anyone directly prominent in the king's service. After an execution, everything is quiet in a few hours, and the incident seems forgotten. The African Negro's attitude towards the whole affair seems to be instinctive, and as long as he escapes he does not show any particular concern in his fellow man. His is of an animal instinctive nature.

"The males of the African tribes of savages have very little respect for a woman, but they demand a whole lot of courtesies from their wives, beating them unmercifully when they feel proper respect has not been shown them. The men hunt game and make war on other tribes, and the women do all the work. A savage warrior, when not engaged in hunting or war, sleeps a lot and smokes almost continuously during his waking hours. Girls are bought from their parents while mere children by the payment of so many cows, goats, etc. The king can take any woman of the tribe—whether married or single—he desires to be his wife. The parents of young girls taken to wife by the king of a tribe feel honored and fall on their knees and thank the king for taking her.

"The prince of a tribe is born a headsman, and as soon as he is able to wield a knife he is called upon to perform the duty of cutting off the heads of criminals who are condemned to death by the king for general crimes. Those condemned by the witch doctor for witchcraft are executed by dismemberment or fire as described above.

"My husband was a cannibal headsman and performed this duty of cutting off persons' heads when a boy, and after being civilized in America this feature of his early life bore so heavily upon his mind that it was instrumental in driving him insane. By custom, a prince was born a headsman, and it was compulsory that he execute criminals. He died in an insane ward of the New Jersey State Hospital."

MARY REYNOLDS

Born: 1837
Age: 100
Master: Dr. Kilpatrick
Place: Black River, Louisiana
Interviewer: Heloise Foreman
Source: Second Supplemental Series, Texas Narratives,
   volume 08T, page 3284

Mary Reynolds claims to be more than a hundred years old. She was born in slavery to the Kilpatrick family in Black River, Louisiana. Mary now lives at the Dallas County Convalescent Home. She has been blind for five years and is very feeble.

"My paw's name was Tom Vaughn, and he was from the North, born a free man and lived and died free to the end of his days. He wasn't no eddicated man, but he was what he calls himself a piano man. He told me once he lived in New York and Chicago, and he built the insides of pianos and knew how to make them play in tune. He said some white folks from the South told he if he'd come with them to the South he'd find a lot of work to do with pianos in them parts, and he come off with them.

"He saw my maw on the Kilpatrick place, and her man was dead. He told Dr. Kilpatrick, my massa, he'd buy my maw and her three chillun with all the money he had, iffen he'd sell her. But Dr. Kilpatrick was never one to sell any but the old niggers who was past workin' in the fields and past their breedin' times. So my paw marries my maw and works the fields, same as any other nigger. They had six gals—Martha and Pamela and Josephine and Ellen and Katherine and me.

"I was born same time as Miss Sara Kilpatrick. Dr. Kilpatrick's first wife and my maw come to their time right together. Miss Sara's maw died, and they brung Miss Sara to suck with me. It's a thing we ain't never forgot. My maw's name was Sallie, and Miss Sara allus looked with kindness on my maw.

"We sucked till we was a fair size and played together, which wasn't no common thing. None the other li'l niggers played with the white chillun. But Miss Sara loved me so good.

"I was just 'bout big nuff to start playin' with a broom to go 'bout sweepin' up and not even half doin' it when Dr. Kilpatrick sold me. They was a old white man in Trinity, and his wife died, and he didn't have chick or child or slave or nothin'. Massa sold me cheap 'cause he didn't want Miss Sara to play with no nigger youngun. That old man bought me a big doll and went off and left me all day with the door open. I just sat on the floor and played with that doll. I used to cry. He'd come home and give me somethin' to eat and then go to bed, and I slept on the foot of the bed with him. I was scairt all the time in the dark. He never did close the door.

"Miss Sara pined and sickened. Massa done what he could, but they wasn't no pertness in her. She got sicker and sicker, and Massa brung 'nother doctor. He say, 'You li'l gal is grievin' the life out her body, and she sho gwine die iffen you don't do somethin' 'bout it.' Miss Sara says over and over, 'I wants Mary.'

Massa say to the doctor, 'That a li'l nigger youngun I done sold.' The doctor tells him he better get me back iffen he wants to save the life of his child. Dr. Kilpatrick has to give a big plenty more to get me back than what he sold me for, but Miss Sara plumps up right off and grows into fine health.

"Then Massa marries a rich lady from Mississippi, and they has chillun for company to Miss Sara, and seem like for a time she forgets me.

"Massa Kilpatrick wasn't no piddlin' man. He was a man of plenty. He had a big house with no more style to it than a crib, but it could room plenty people. He was a medicine doctor, and they was rooms in the second story for sick folks what come to lay in. It would take two days to go all over the land he owned. He had cattle and stock and sheep and more'n a hundred slaves and more besides. He bought the best of niggers near every time the speculators come that way. He'd make a swap of the old ones and give money for young ones what could work.

"He raised corn and cotton and cane and taters and goobers, 'sides the peas and other feedin' for the niggers. I 'member I held a hoe handle mighty unsteady when they put a old women to learn me and some other chillun to scrape the fields. That old woman would be in a frantic. She'd show me and then turn 'bout to show some other li'l nigger, and I'd have the young corn cut clean as the grass. She say, 'For the love of Gawd, you better learn it right or Solomon will beat the breath out you body.' Old man Solomon was the nigger driver.

"Slavery was the worst days was ever seed in the world. They was things past tellin', but I got the scars on my old body to show to this day. I seed worse than what happened to me. I seed them put the men and women in the stock with they hands screwed down through holes in the board and they feets tied together and they naked behinds to the world. Solomon the overseer beat them with a big whip, and Massa look on. The niggers better not stop in the fields when they hear them yellin'. They cut the flesh 'most to the bones, and some they was when they taken them out of the stock and put them on the beds, they never got up again.

"When a nigger died, they let his folks come out the fields to see him 'fore he died. They buried him the same day. They take a big plank and bust it with a ax in the middle nuff to bend it back, and put the dead nigger in betwixt it. They'd cart them down to the graveyard on the place and not bury them deep nuff that buzzards wouldn't come circlin' round. Niggers mourns now, but in them days they wasn't no time for mournin'.

"The conch shell blowed 'fore daylight, and all hands better get out for roll call or Solomon bust the door down and get them out. It was work hard, get beatin's, and [be] half-fed. They brung the victuals and water to the fields on a slide pulled by a old mule. Plenty times, they was only a half-barrel water, and it stale and hot, for all us niggers on the hottest days. Mostly, we ate pickled pork and cornbread and peas and beans and taters. They never was as much as we needed.

"The times I hated most was pickin' cotton when the frost was on the bolls. My hands get sore and crack open and bleed. We'd have a li'l fire in the fields, and iffen the ones with tender hands couldn't stand it no longer we'd run and warm our hands a li'l bit. When I could steal a tater, I used to slip it in the ashes, and when I'd run to the fire I'd take it out and eat it on the sly.

"In the cabins, it was nice and warm. They was built of pine boardin', and they was one long row of them up the hill back of the big house. Near one side of the cabins was a fireplace. They'd bring in two, three big logs and put on the fire, and they'd last near a week. The beds was made out of puncheons fitted in holes bored in the wall and planks laid 'cross them poles. We had tickin' mattresses filled with corn shucks. Sometimes, the men build chairs at night. We didn't know much 'bout havin' nothin', though.

"Sometimes, Massa let niggers have a li'l patch. They'd raise taters or goobers. They liked to have them to help fill out on the victuals. Taters roasted in the ashes was the best-tastin' eatin' I ever had. I could die better satisfied to have just one more tater roasted in hot ashes. The niggers had to work the patches at night and dig the taters and goobers at night. Then if they wanted to sell any in town, they'd have to get a pass to go. They had to go at night 'cause they couldn't ever spare a hand from the fields.

"Once in a while, they'd give us a li'l piece of Sat'day evenin' to wash out clothes in the branch. We hanged them in the woods to dry. They was a place to wash clothes from the well, but they was so many niggers all couldn't get round to it on Sundays. When they'd get through with the clothes on Sat'day evenin's, the niggers which sold they goobers and taters brung fiddles and guitars and come out and play. The others clap they hands and stomp they feet, and we younguns cut a step round. I liked to cut a step.

"We was scairt of Solomon and his whip, though, and he didn't like frolickin'. He didn't like for us niggers to pray either. We never heared of no church, but us have prayin' in the cabins. We'd set on the floor and pray with our heads down low and sing low, but if Solomon heared he'd come and beat on the wall with the stock of his whip. He'd say, 'I'll come in there and tear the hide off you backs.' But some the old niggers tell us we got to pray to Gawd that he don't think different of the blacks and the whites. I know that Solomon is burnin' in hell today, and it pleasures me to know it.

"Once, my maw and paw taken me and Katherine after night to slip to 'nother place to a prayin' and singin'. A nigger man with white beard told us a day am comin' when niggers only be slaves of Gawd. We prays for the end of trib'lation and the end of beatin's and shoes that fit our feet. We prayed that us niggers could have all we wanted to eat, and special for fresh meat. Some the old ones say we have to bear all, 'cause that all we can do. Some say they was glad to [look forward to] the time they's dead, 'cause they'd rather rot in the ground than have the beatin's. What I hated most was when they'd beat me and I didn't know what they beat me for, and I hated them strippin' me naked as the day I was born.

"When we's comin' back from the prayin', I think I heared the nigger dogs and somebody on horseback. I say, 'Maw, it's them nigger hounds, and they'll eat us up.' You could hear them old hounds a-bayin'. Maw listens and say, 'Sho nuff, them dogs am runnin', and Gawd help us!' Then she and Paw talk, and they take us to a fence corner and stands us up 'gainst the rails and say, 'Don't move, and if anyone comes near don't breathe loud.' They went to the woods so the hounds chase them and not get us. Me and Katherine stand there holdin' hands, shakin' so we can hardly stand. We hears the hounds come nearer, but we don't move. They goes after Paw and Maw, but they circles round to the cabins and gets in. Maw say it's the power of Gawd.

"In them days, I weared shirts like all the younguns. They had collars and come below the knees and was split up the sides. That's all we weared in hot weather. The men weared jeans and the women gingham. Shoes was the worstest trouble. We weared rough russets [shoes made of hide] when it got cold, and it seem powerful strange they'd never get them to fit. Once when I was a young gal, they got me a new pair and all brass studs in the toes.

They was too li'l for me, but I had to wear them. The brass trimmin's cut into my ankles, and them places got mis'ble bad. I rubs tallow in them sore places and wraps rags round them, and my sores got worser and worser. The scars are there to this day.

"I wasn't sick much, though. Some the niggers had chills and fever a lot, but they hadn't discovered so many diseases then as now. Dr. Kilpatrick give sick niggers ipecac and asafetida and oil and turpentine and black fever pills.

"They was a cabin called the spinnin' house, and two looms and two spinnin' wheels goin' all the time, and two nigger women sewing all the time. It took plenty sewin' to make all the things for a place so big. Once, Massa goes to Baton Rouge and brung back a yeller gal dressed in fine style. She was a seamster nigger. He builds her a house 'way from the quarters, and she done fine sewin' for the whites. Us niggers knowed the doctor took a black woman quick as he did a white, and took any on his place he wanted, and he took them often. But mostly the chillun born on the place looked like niggers. Aunt Cheyney allus say four of hers was Massa's, but he didn't give them no mind. But this yeller gal breeds so fast and gets a mess of white younguns. She learnt them fine manners and combs out they hair.

"Once, two of them goes down the hill to the dollhouse where the Kilpatrick chillun am playin'. They wants to go in the dollhouse, and one the Kilpatrick boys say, 'That's for white chillun.' They say, 'We ain't no niggers 'cause we got the same daddy you has, and he comes to see us near every day and fetches us clothes and things from town.' They is fussin', and Missy Kilpatrick is listenin' out her chamber window. She heard them white niggers say, 'He is our daddy, and we call him Daddy when he comes to our house to see our mama.'

"When Massa come home that evenin', his wife hardly say nothin' to him, and he ask her what the matter, and she tells him, 'Since you asks me, I'm studyin' in my mind 'bout them white younguns of that yeller nigger wench from Baton Rouge.' He say, 'Now, honey, I fetches that gal just for you 'cause she a fine seamster.' She say, 'It look kind of funny they got the same kind of hair and eyes as my chillun, and they got a nose looks like yours.' He say, 'Honey, you just payin' 'tention to talk of li'l chillun that ain't got no mind to what they say.' She say, 'Over in Mississippi, I got a home and plenty with my daddy, and I got that in my mind.'

"Well, she didn't never leave, and Massa bought her a fine new span of surrey hosses. But she don't never have no more chillun, and she ain't so cordial with the massa. Margaret, that yeller gal, has more white younguns, but they don't never go down the hill no more to the big house.

"Aunt Cheyney was just out of bed with a sucklin' baby one time, and she run away. Some say that was 'nother baby of Massa's breedin'. She don't come to the house to nurse her baby, so they misses her, and old Solomon gets the nigger hounds and takes her trail. They gets near her, and she grabs a limb and tries to hoist herself in a tree, but them dogs grab her and pull her down. The men hollers them onto her, and the dogs tore her naked and et the breasts plum off her body. She got well and lived to be a old woman, but 'nother woman has to suck her baby, and she ain't got no sign of breasts no more.

"They give all the niggers fresh meat on Christmas and a plug tobacco all round. The highest cotton picker gets a suit of clothes, and all the women what had twins that year gets a outfittin' of clothes for the twins and a double warm blanket.

"Seems like after I got bigger, I 'member more and more niggers run away. They's most allus catched. Massa used to hire out his niggers for wage hands. One time, he hired me and a nigger boy, Turner, to work for some ornery white trash name of Kidd.

One day, Turner goes off and don't come back. Old man Kidd say I knowed 'bout it, and he tied my wrists together and stripped me. He hanged me by the wrists from a limb on a tree and straddled my legs round the trunk and tied my feet together. Then he beat me. He beat me worser than I ever been beat before, and I faints dead away. When I come to, I'm in bed. I didn't care so much iffen I died.

"I didn't know 'bout the passin' of time, but Miss Sara come to me. Some white folks done get word to her. Mr. Kidd tries to talk hisself out of it, but Miss Sara fetches me home when I'm well nuff to move. She took me in a cart, and my maw takes care of me. Massa looks me over good and says I'll get well, but I'm ruin for breedin' chillun.

"After while, I taken a notion to marry, and Massa and Missy marries us same as all the niggers. They stands inside the house with a broom held crosswise in the door, and we stands outside. Missy puts a li'l wreath on my head they kept near, and we steps over the broom into the house. Now, that's all they was to marryin'. After freedom, I gets married and has it put in the book by a preacher.

"One day, we was workin' in the fields and hears the conch shell blow, so we all goes to the back gate of the big house. Massa am there. He say, 'Call the toll for every nigger big nuff to walk, and I wants them to go to the river and wait there. They's gwine be a show, and I wants you to see it.' They was a big boat down there, done built up on the sides with boards and holes in the boards and a big gun barrel stickin' through every hole. We ain't never seed nothin' like that. Massa goes up the plank onto the boat and comes out on the boat porch. He say, 'This am a Yankee boat.' He goes inside, and the waterwheels starts movin', and that boat goes movin' up the river, and they says it goes to Natchez.

"The boat wasn't more'n out of sight when a big drove of soldiers comes into town. They say they's Federals. More'n half the niggers goes off with them soldiers, but I goes on back home 'cause of my old mammy.

"Next day, them Yankees is swarmin' the place. Some the niggers wants to show them somethin'. I follows to the woods. The niggers shows them soldiers a big pit in the ground, bigger'n a big house. It is got wooden doors that lifts up, but the top am sodded and grass growin' on it, so you couldn't tell it. In that pit is stock—hosses and cows and mules—and money and chinaware and silver and a mess of stuff them soldiers takes.

"We just sat on the place doin' nothin' till the white folks comes home. Miss Sara come out to the cabin and say she wants to read a letter to my mammy. It come from Louis Carter, which is brother to my mammy, and he done follow the Federals to Galveston. A white man done write the letter for him. It am tored in half, and Massa done that. The letter say Louis am workin' in Galveston and wants Mammy to come with us, and he'll pay our way. Miss Sara say Massa swear, 'Damn Louis Carter. I ain't gwine tell Sallie nothin',' and he starts to tear the letter up. But she won't let him, and she reads it to Mammy.

"After a time, Massa takes all his niggers what wants to Texas with him, and Mammy gets to Galveston and dies there. I goes with Massa to the Tennessee colony and then to Navasota [Texas]. Miss Sara marries Mr. T. Coleman and goes to El Paso. She wrote and told me to come to her, and I allus meant to go.

"My husband and me farmed round for times, and then I done housework and cookin' for many years. I come to Dallas and cooked seven year for one white family. My husband died years ago. I guess Miss Sara been dead these long years. I allus kept my years by Miss Sara's years, 'count we is born so close.

"I been blind and 'most helpless for five year. I'm gettin' mighty enfeeblin', and I ain't walked outside the door for a long time back. I sets and 'members the times in the world. I 'members now clear as yesterday things I forgot for a long time. I 'members 'bout the days of slavery, and I don't believe they ever gwine have slaves no more on this earth. I think Gawd done took that offen his black chillun, and I'm aimin' to praise Him for it to His face in the days of glory what ain't so far off."

VALLEY PERRY

Born: 1887
Age: Fifty
Master: None
Place: Wake County, North Carolina
Interviewer: Mary Hicks
Source: First Series, Library of Congress Rare Book Room
    Collection, North Carolina Narratives, volume 15A,
    page 167

"Course, bein' no older dan I is, I can't recollect 'bout de war, but I's heard my mammy tell a little an' my granmammy tell a right smart 'bout dem slavery times you's talkin' 'bout.

"Granmammy Josephine an' Mammy Clarice 'longed to a Mr. Nat Whitaker in Wake County. Mr. Nat's wife was named Missus Lucy, an' she was so good dat everybody what ever seed her 'membered her. Dere is even de belief among de niggers dat she rise up to heaven alive, like Elijah.

"Dey said dat Mr. Nat's overseer was kinda mean to de slaves, an' when he whupped 'em dey 'membered it to de longest day dey lived. Mr. Nat wasn't near so bad, an' Miz Lucy was a angel. She'd beg Mr. Nat to make de overseer stop, but Mr. Nat 'fused 'cause he said dat de niggers won't obey him iffen he teaches 'em he won't let de overseer punish 'em good an' plenty. Then Miz Lucy'd cry, an' she'd run an' grab de overseer's arm an' beg him to stop. She'd cry so hard dat he'd hafter stop.

"Finally, de overseer goes to Mr. Nat an' complains, an' he says dat he am gwine to quit de job iffen Mr. Nat don't make Miz Lucy keep outen his business. Mr. Nat ask him to tell him 'fore he starts to beat 'em, an' to set a time for de beatin', an' dat he will get Miz Lucy offen de place.

"Well, de overseer does what Mr. Nat says an' waits to whup everybody on Tuesday, an' on Tuesday Mr. Nat takes Miz Lucy to town. Miz Lucy am tickled pink dat she am a-goin' shoppin', an' she ain't suspicion nothin' at all. When she gets to shoppin', though, she ain't satisfied, an' terribly she tells Mr. Nat dat she wants to go home. Mr. Nat tries to get her to go to a concert, but Miz Lucy says no, dat she feels like somethin' am happenin' at home. Mr. Nat begs her to stay on an' enjoy herself, but when she won't listen to no reason at all he starts home. De mules creep an' poke, but Miz Lucy herself whups 'em up, an' dey gets home sooner dan dey am expected.

"When dey drives up in de yard, de overseer am so busy whuppin' de niggers what has done bad dat he ain't seed Miz Lucy till she am right on him, den she snatch de heavy bullwhip, an' she strikes him two or three times right in de face. Miz Lucy look delicate, but she cuts de blood outen his cheek an' she shets up one of his eyes an' brings de blood a-pourin' from his nose. Den de meek little woman draws back de whup again, an' she 'lows, 'Get offen dis plantation, an' iffen ever I catches you here again I'll shoot you, you beast.'

"Dat settled de overseer's hash, an' after he left Miz Lucy went to doctorin'. Granmammy said dat dere wasn't no more trouble wid de niggers, an' Miz Lucy done all of de punishin' herself. She made de meanest ones learn a whole passel of scripture. She punish de chillun by makin' 'em memorize poems an' such. Sometimes she sent 'em to bed widout supper, sometimes she make 'em work at night, sometimes she prayed for 'em, an' once in a coon's age she whupped. Dey said dat she could really hurt when she meant to, but she whupped as de last thing to do, an' she whupped wid a little switch 'stead of de leather.

"Once after she had whupped a little nigger, she said, 'Clarice, dis hurt me wusser dan it did yo'.' Clarice look at Miz Lucy, then she says, 'Iffen it hurt yo' wusser dan it did me, I's powerful sorry for you.' Dat little gal was my mammy.

"My granfather was named Jake, an' he 'longed to a family by de name of Middleton somewhere in de neighborhood.

"Marse Nat ain't had no use for Mr. Middleton 'cause he tried to act up, an' he was a New York Yankee to boot, what thought that he owned de heavens an' de earth. When Granfather Jake fell in love wid Granmammy, nobody ain't knowed it 'cause dere marsters am mad at each other, an' dey knows dat dere won't be no marryin' 'twixt de families.

"Time goes on, an' Granfather runs away an' comes to see Granmammy, but one night Mr. Middleton follers Granfather an' finds him in Granmammy cabin.

"Mr. Middleton don't wait to say nothin' to nobody when he peeps in at de winder an' sees 'em a-settin' at de table eatin' muskmelons what Granpappy had stole outen his patch. He just comes in a-rarin' an' a-tearin' an' starts a-whuppin' wid his ridin' quirt. He whups Granfather for a while, den he pitches in on Granmammy.

"While all dis am a-goin' on, somebody runs for Marster Nat, an' when he gets dere dere am trouble in de shack. Marse Nat ain't so heavy as Mr. Middleton, but man, he puts de beatin' on Mr. Middleton, den he makes him sell Jake to him, an' he pays him spot cash right den an' dere.

"De next day, he thinks to ask Granmammy what Jake am a-doin' in her cabin, an' Granmammy tells him dat she loves Jake an' dat she wants to marry him. Marse Nat laugh fit to kill, an' he says dat dey'll have a big weddin' at de house for 'em.

"Dey did have a big weddin', an' Granmammy wore a red dress dat Miz Lucy give her. She said dat she wish dat Granfather could of wore red, too.

"She said dat when Mammy was borned dat ol' Dr. Freeman 'tended her an' dat she stayed in de bed two weeks. Miz Lucy was good to de niggers like dat.

"I 'members Granmammy tellin' 'bout de Yankees comin', an' how she stood front of Miz Lucy's door wid de ax an' told 'em dat she'd chop out anybody's brains what tried to go in. De door was open, an' dey could see Miz Lucy a-settin' dere white as a sheet, so dey went on searchin' for valuables, an' all de time dem valuables was in Miz Lucy's room."

MAGGIE WESMOLAND

Born: 1852
Age: Eighty-five
Master: Unknown
Place: Prairie County, Arkansas
Interviewer: Irene Robertson
Source: First Series, Library of Congress Rare Book Room
    Collection, Arkansas Narratives, volume 11A,
        page 99

"I was born in Arkansas in slavery time beyond Des Arc. My parents was sold in Mississippi. They was brought to Arkansas. I never seed my father after the closing of the war. He had been refugeed to Texas and come back here, then he went on back to Mississippi. Mama had seventeen children. She had six by my stepfather. When my stepfather was mustered out at Duval's Bluff, he come to Miz Holland's and got Mama and took her on wid him. I was give to Miz Holland's daughter. She married a Cargo. The Hollands raised me and my sister. I never seen Mama after she left. My mother was Jane Holland, and my father was Smith Woodson. They lived on different places here in Arkansas. I had a hard time. I was awfully abused by the old man that married Miss Betty. She was my young mistress. He was poor and hated Negroes. He said they didn't have no feeling.

He drank all the time. He never had been used to Negroes, and he didn't like 'em. He was a middle-age man, but Miss Betty Holland was in her teens.

"No, Mama didn't have as hard a time as I had. She was Miz Holland's cook and washwoman. Miss Betty told her old husband, 'Papa don't beat his Negroes. He is good to his Negroes.' He worked overseers in the field. Nothing Miss Betty ever told him done a bit of good. He didn't have no feeling. I had to go in a trot all the time. I was scared to death of him, he beat me so. I'm scarred up all over now where he lashed me. He would strip me stark naked and tie my hands crossed and whup me till the blood ooze out and drip on the ground when I walked. The flies blowed [infected] me time and again.

"Miss Betty catch him gone, would grease my places and put turpentine on them to kill the places blowed. He kept a bundle of hickory switches at the house all the time. Miss Betty was good to me. She would cry and beg him to be good to me.

"One time, the cow kicked over my milk. I was scared not to take some milk to the house, so I went to the spring and put some water in the milk. He was snooping round spying somewhere and seen me. He beat me nearly to death. I never did know what suit him and what wouldn't. Didn't nothing please him. He was a poor man, never been used to nothin', and took spite on me everything happened. They didn't have no children while I was there, but he did have a boy before he died. He died 'fore I left Dardanelle. When Miss Betty Holland married Mr. Cargo, she lived close to Dardanelle. That is where he was so mean to me. He lived in the deer- and bear-hunting country.

"Two men come there deer hunting every year. One time, he had beat me before them, and on their way home they went to the Freedmen's Bureau and told how he beat me and what he done it for—biggetness. He was a biggety-acting and braggy-talking old man. When he got to town, they asked him if he wasn't hiding a little Negro girl, ask if he sent me to school. He come home. I slept on a bed made down at the foot of their bed. That night, he told his wife what all he said and what all they ask him. He said he would kill whoever come there bothering about me. He been telling that about. He told Miss Betty they would fix me up and let me go stay a week at my sister's Christmas. He went back to town, bought me the first shoes I had had since they took me. They was brogan shoes. They put a pair of his sock on me. Miss Betty made the calico dress for me and made a body out of some of his pants legs and quilted the skirt part, bound it at the bottom with red flannel. She made my things nice—put my underskirt in a little frame and quilted it so it would be warm. Christmas day was a bright, warm day. In the morning when Miss Betty dressed me up, I was so proud. He started me off and told me how to go.

"I got to the big creek. I got down in the ditch—couldn't get across. I was running up and down it looking for a place to cross. A big old mill was up on the hill. I could see it. I seen three men coming—a white man with a gun and two Negro men on horses or mules. I heard one say, 'Yonder she is.' Another said, 'It don't look like her.' One said, 'Call her.' One said, 'Margaret.' I answered. They come to me and said, 'Go to the mill and cross on a foot log.' I went up there and crossed and got up on a stump behind my brother-in-law on his horse. I didn't know him. The white man was the man he was sharecroppin' with. They all lived in a big yard close together. I hadn't seen my sister before in about four years. Mr. Cargo told me if I wasn't back at his house New Year's Day he would come after me on his horse and run me every step of the way home. It was nearly twenty-five miles. He said he would give me the worst whupping I ever got in my life. I was going back, scared not to be back. Had no other place to live.

"When New Year's Day come, the white man locked me up in a room in his house, and I stayed in there two days. They brought me plenty to eat. I slept in there with their children. Mr. Cargo never come after me till March. He didn't see me when he come. It started in raining and cold, and the roads was bad. When he come in March, I seen him. I knowed him. I lay down and covered up in leaves. They was deep. I had been in the woods getting sweet gum when I seen him. He scared me. He never seen me. This white man bound me to his wife's friend for a year to keep Mr. Cargo from getting me back. The woman at the house and Mr. Cargo had war nearly about me. I missed my whuppings. I never got none that whole year. It was Missus Brown, twenty miles from Dardanelle, they bound me over to. I never got no more than the common run of Negro children, but they wasn't mean to me.

"When I was at Cargo's, he wouldn't buy me shoes. Miss Betty would have, but in them days the man was head of his house. Miss Betty made me moccasins to wear out in the snow—made them out of old rags and pieces of his pants. I had risings [blisters] on my feet, and my feet frostbit till they was solid sores. He would take his knife and stab my risings to see the matter pop way out. The ice cut my feet. He cut my foot on the side with a cowhide nearly to the bone. [When] Miss Betty catch him outer sight, [she] would doctor my feet. Seem like she was scared of him. He wasn't none too good to her.

"He told his wife the Freedmen's Bureau said turn that Negro girl loose. She didn't want me to leave her. He despised nasty Negroes, he said. One of them fellows what come for me had been to Cargo's and seen me. He was the Negro man come to show Patsy's husband and his sharecropper where I was at. He whupped me twice before them deer hunters. They visited him every spring and fall hunting deer, but they reported him to the Freedmen's Bureau. They knowed he was showing off.

"He overtook me on a horse one day four or five years after I left there. I was on my way from school. I was grown. He wanted me to come back and live with them. Said Miss Betty wanted to see me so bad. I was so scared I lied to him and said yes to all he said. He wanted to come get me a certain day. I lied about where I lived. He went to the wrong place to get me, I heard. I was afraid to meet him on the road. He died at Dardanelle before I come 'way from there.

"After I got grown, I hired out cooking at $1.25 a week and then $1.50 a week. When I was a girl, I plowed some. I worked in the field a mighty little, but I have done a mountain of washing and ironing in my life. I can't tell you to save my life what a hard time I had when I was growing up. My daughter is a blessing to me. She is so good to me.

"I never knowed nor seen the Ku Klux. The bushwhackers was awful after the war. They went about stealing, and they wouldn't work.

"Conditions is far better for young folks now than when I come on. They can get chances I couldn't get. My daughter is tied down here with me. She could do washings and ironings if she could get them and do it here at home. I think she got one give over to her for a while. The regular washwoman is sick. It is hard for me to get a living since I been sick. I get commodities. But the diet I am on, it is hard to get it. The money is the trouble. I had two strokes, and I been sick with high blood pressure three years. We own our house. Times is all right if I was able to work and enjoy things. I don't get the old-age pension, I reckon because my daughter's husband has a job. I reckon that is it. I can't hardly buy milk, that is the main thing. The doctor told me to eat plenty milk.

"I never voted."

SILVIA KING

Born: c. 1804
Age: c. 133
Master: Mr. Jones
Place: Orleans County, Louisiana
Interviewer: Mrs. Wade Davis
Source: Second Supplemental Series, Texas Narratives,
    volume 06T, page 2224

Silvia King, French Negress of Marlin, Texas, does not know her age but says that she was born in Morocco. She was stolen from her husband and three children, brought to the United States, and sold into slavery. Silvia has the appearance of extreme age and may be over a hundred years old, as she thinks she is, because of her memories of the children she never saw again and of the slave ship.

"De white folks say dat I was borned in Morocco, Africa, on Christmas day 1804. I don't know in what part of dat country. I was took to France, an' dere I married. I had three chillun. I was stole from my husband and chillun an' sold. First, dey took me from Africa to France, an' from Bordeaux, France,

I was stole an' drugged wid some coffee an' put down in chains in de bottom of a boat wid a whole lot of other niggers.

"De ship, it come to dis country to New Orleans, an' dere I was put on de block an' sold. Yes'm, I knows how dey done on de block. All de blacks was chained, an' all dere clothes was stripped off when dey was gettin' 'em ready for de block. Dey all—chillun, women, an' men—had to stand on a big wooden block like de butcher man chops an' saws he meat on nowadays. De folks what was gwine to buy de niggers, dey come round an' pinch you an' feel of your body all over, an' look for scars an' see you got any broken bones 'fore dey buy you. Iffen any of de niggers don't want to take their clothes off, de overseer, he get a long black whip an' cut 'em up hard. I was sold to a planter who had him a big plantation in Fayette County, Texas. Don't know no name 'cept Marse Jones. He had de meanest man in de States as overseer. Dat man was name Smith, an' he boasts 'bout how many niggers he kilt.

"De white man, when he see me, say, 'Dat's a whale of a woman.' Den he look me all over, an' some other man want me, but I's so scairt, an' I can't speak English, so he bought me. Marse Jones, he awful good to me.

"Dey chain us togedder an' march us to Fayette County, near La Grange. Dat was an awful time. All I 'member was dat we marched 'long togedder, an' when us come to a stream of water an' one gets a drink, all us had to do dat. Iffen one get tired or sick, de rest just had to drag an' carry dat one. But when us get to Texas, old Marse, he raise de debbil wid dat white man what had us on de march. He get he doctor man, an' he tell he cook to feed us, an' he say us got to rest up.

"Texas was a wilderness where us den gwine to. De white folkses an' de Mexicans fit an' fit hard. An' den dey say dat Texas ain't be bossed by de Mexican general no more. When I gets to de Fayette County place, Marse, he say, 'Silvia, you gwine get married.' I tells him I got a man back in de old country, but he don't understand my language, an' I don't understand his'n, an' dere I was. I scairt to death, don't know what gwine happen next. Oh, I don't bother wid dat black man's name, he just Bob. But I fit him good an' plenty till de overseer, he shake a black-snake whip over me.

"After I cooked in de cabin in de quarters awhile, de marster, he an' ol' Miss, dey find out 'bout my cookin', an' den I's took to de big house. De dishes an' things was awful queer to what I been brung up to use in France. 'Bout time I had my first chile in dis country, ol' Marse, he 'cided to move an' get him more land. He allus say he gwine to get where he cain't hear de neighbor's cow horn.

"I was a powerful big woman when I was young, an' when dey get in tight in de work, I help out.

"De place in Fayette County where us move to was just all woods an' grassland—no houses, no roads, no bridges, no neighbors, nothin' but de woods and wild animals. Yes'm, dat sho was a mighty fine house Marse had built. De chimbley was made of stone dat de servants gathered here an' yon. It musta been six foot square down at de bottom. De sill of dat house was a foot square, an' den dey split out two-inch plank from de trees, an' after dey made de room outen de logs dey put dese here smoothed-off planks on de outside from de ground almost clear up to de eaves. No'm, dere wasn't no nails like nowadays. Dey whittled out pegs an' fasten dem walls an' things wid dem pegs 'stead of nails. An' dey hold, too, till de whole house rot down. De lumber was hewn at home by de white men an' de servants. Dere was two big rooms wid de upstairs, an' den dere was a ell out de back. Dere was a well on de back porch by de kitchen door. It had a wheel an' rope. Dere was a well by de barns an' one or two round de quarters. In de kitchen was a big fireplace. Dere was big back logs hauled in to de doors of de big house every once an' so often. De oxen pulled 'em dat far, an' den several men took poles an' roll 'em in place. Marse never let de fire go out from October till de next May. In de fall, Marse, or one of he sons light de fire wid a flint rock an' powder.

"De stores was a long way off. De folkses, de white folkses, dey would loan seed an' grain to one anudder. When dere was a rush of de work, one man would hire out he servants to anudder man what needed help. Dere was a black man on de plantation dat shod de horses an' de oxen, made door an' gate hinges an' such. He allus had him one or two of de younger boys, learnin' 'em how to do his work. De blacksmith would pull a tooth iffen it had to be done, but most in general, de servants, dey didn't have no teeth pulled. De blacksmith, he fixed de plows an' de other tools an' de harness an' such. Marse had two what dey call in dem days five-cattle team. Dat was where you work two yokes of oxen an' a hoss togedder. Marse could hire 'em out most anytime. Ol' Jock an' my husband, dey manage dem kinda teams. I was a household slave an' a cook most all de time. But I managed de garden. Miss had a flower garden, an' she kept two niggers busy in it all de time. Make no difference how busy de field or de wood get or de cattle, she gwine keep dem niggers right dere. She sure had a purty place, too. An' den de orchard. It was a big one an' a fine one. In de different fruit seasons, all de women on de place were workin' from 'fore daylight till late at night, dryin' an' preservin' an' de like. It took a lot of fruit an' things to feed de fambly an' de servants.

"An' my ol' marse an' mistress, dey gwine feed you an' see dat de quarters be dry and warm an' look after you when you sick, or dey gonna know de reason why.

"Marse an' Miss, most every night, one or t'other of 'em

make de rounds of de cabins an' see iffen any servant be sick. De nigger was worth a lot of money in dem times. All through de year, dey kill a beef when dey needed it, or a hog. Down in Fayette County, when dey kill a beef, most all de time dey just keep de choice cuts an' throw de other away. In de fall, us had what dey call de hog-killin' time. Everybody work hard, but everybody had plenty to eat. An' de preacher man, he tell us how to get to de fellom city [heaven] and see de ring lights [bright lights]. An' de smokehouse, it full of bacon sides an' cured hams an' barrels of 'lasses an' lard. Every time a nigger want to eat, all he do is just ask an' get his passel [portion] out.

"Miss allus 'pended on me to spice de ham when it get cured. I learned dat back in de ol' country, in France.

"Dere was servants what tanned de hides of de cows to make de leather. De cobbler had he log cabin an' cobbler's bench, just like dere was cabins wid de spinning wheels an' looms in 'em. Dey was big, long cabins wid a chimbley in each end. Us women spun de thread an' wove de cloth for all de clothes for de servants an' for Marse's fambly an' de big house. I's de cook, but sometimes I hit de spinnin' wheel an' de loom fairly well. Us bleached de cloth us wove at home an' den dyed it in blocks, stripes, an' all-over colors.

"Dere was allus a big woodpile in de yard. When dey wasn't doin' nothin', Marse had de men cut wood for winter. Dere was a big caboose kettle in de yard dat was used for renderin' hog fat an' beef tallow for candles, an' it was used for makin' soap. Dere was a big hopper or two standin' round back of de houses, an' us put de wood ashes in 'em an' made lye to make soap outen. Marse allus had de servants to take some of de apples and make cider. An' he made beer at home, too. Most everybody on de plantation had cider an' beer when dey wanted it, but nobody got drunk; Marse sho cut up 'bout dat. I don't 'member 'bout no whiskey. Seems like dat's newfangled stuff. Ol' Miss had some of her rooms sanded. Oh, dat's where you sprinkled fine white sand all over de floor, an' den you sweep it round in all kinds of purty figures. Us made our broom outen corn shucks an' little limber willow twigs an' other kinds of twigs an' outen what dey call de broom weed. Den dere was a littler pot. It was just to dye cloth in. Us made de work clothes outen linsey-woolsey dat was two threads of cotton an' one of wool. Lots of de white men had leather britches iffen dey was hunters. Marse was sho a fool 'bout he hounds, an' he had a mighty fine pack.

"De young boys both black an' white had big times huntin' wolves, painters [panthers], bear, an' other wild game. Folks had lots of wild turkey, an' dere was droves of wild prairie chickens. An' de chilluns would get birds' eggs. An' my, de fish. Every chance I has all my life, I's loved to fish, an' dey do say dat I's a champeen. Den dere was rabbit an' squirrel an' Indian puddin'—dat was made of cornmeal. Nowadays, folkses don't cook nuff wid cornmeal. Why, I's baked many a cake wid cornmeal, an' it tasted real tasty. An' den us et goose, pork, mutton, beef, bear meat, deer, an' den de pies, apple dumplin's, fritters, milk, butter, homemade cheese, 'lasses, gingerbread, doughnuts, cookies, vegetables, an', oh, I just can't 'member all dem good things us had in dem days. Sho wish us had 'em now. Dey didn't have no oranges 'cept at Christmastime.

"I's sat many a time for hours spinnin' wid two threads, one of 'em in one hand an' de other thread in de other hand, one of my foots on de wheel to keep it movin' an' a baby sleepin' on my lap. Many a night in de winter when de nights get long, I has spun a hank or two 'fore I went to bed. At night, de boys an' de ol' mens allus were whittlin', an' it was not just foolishment. Dey whittled traps, wooden spoons, needles to make de nets for de seines, checkers to play wid, sleds, an' lots of things dey used.

Dere wasn't no stores near, an' us all had to make most everything dat us had. Dere wasn't no dolls, store boughten ones. Dey made rag babies outen de cotton waste, ol' clothes, an' such. Sometimes, ol' Miss, she cut one out an' draw a face an' stuff it wid cotton, an' it real perky.

"Most us smoked a pipe. Yes'm, lots of ol' women an' men dat was white smoked de pipe. I likes my pipe right now. I has two clay pipes, an' I keeps 'em under my pillow, an' I don't aims for to let 'em get outen my sight. I use one awhile, an' den de other. I likes my dip of snuff, too. I's been smokin' 'bout a hunnerd years now. It takes two cans of smokin' terbaccy a week to keep me goin'. I lost what teeth I had 'bout, oh, well, a long time ago. In 1920, dere was two baby teeth come through. Dem teeth sho did worry me. I was glad when dey went. I was 116 years old when I cut dem teeth. In de ol' days, us lit our pipes wid a coal from de fire held in stout tongs. Us lit de candles de same way, an' I lightest mine dat way now. I likes candles better dan de newfangled lights.

"In dose days, de folks traveled by hossback, ox wagon, oxcart, an' carriages. He-he! I sho 'members de first rigs dat come to dis country. Dey scairt de hosses an' mules as much as de first automobiles did. Dere weren't many doctors in dem times, but dere was a closet full of simples [home remedies], an' most all de ol' women, white an' black, could go to de woods an' get medicine. Every spring, ol' Miss, she line all de chillun on de plantation up and give 'em a dose of garlic an' rum. De Mexicans brung de smallpox into de country, an' it sho kilt lots of folks. Yes'm, all de chilluns played togedder, white an' black. I's had a dozen at a time rollin' round on de kitchen floor underfoot, black an' white. Dey fished an' hunted togedder, played ball, rode de plow stock iffen dey got a chance, an' get in debbilment all de time. De young servants wore a long kinda shirt till dey got 'bout fourteen years ol', but de white ones on our plantation did just 'bout like dey dress now. Course, some of de white chillun wore de long shirt, too. You couldn't tell a boy from a gal 'cept dere hair. An' wid de black chillun, you could hardly tell 'em apart.

"De young ones was purty handy trappin' quail, partridges, an' squirrel. Dey didn't shoot iffen dey could catch anything some other way, 'cause de powder an' lead was scarce. Dey would catch de deer by makin' a salt lick kinda, an' by watchin' de water holes. Dey use a spring-pole net to catch de wild pigeons an' birds. When somebody find a bee tree, everybody dat could turned loose an' get dat honey. In de winter evenin's, de men an' boys would sit round de fire an' whittle out things or make nets an' seines to fish wid, an' de women would sew or spin or weave, but not much weavin' at night 'cause it was by candlelight or a pine torch, an' dey couldn't see much. De old folks would tell tales, an' de young ones would whittle, patch harness, or pick cotton offen de seed. But dey gwine go to noddin' purty soon. Corn, potatoes, turnips, an' wheat was sold or loaned by de bushel.

"Nobody can't tell me nothin' 'bout dat furniture in dem times. Dere was de one-legged bed us made by fastenin' two poles togedder an' puttin' de other ends in de wall an' fillin' a bed tick wid prairie hay or shucks an' a little cotton. Every summer, you get a new bed iffen you smart, an' dey sho felt good when you work hard all day an' come nighttime. I's worked a pow'ful lot in my lifetime, an' some of it hard an' some not. De day dat I was hunnerd years ol', I put a big tub of water on my haid, took a bucket of water in each hand, an' walk spry as a cricket. Can't anudder woman round me do dat. I outworked every woman in ten miles of me, an' dem young women an' me a hunnerd. Ella Southern—she's de mammy of my great-grandson what I lives wid now—she allus tell folkses dat I can do mo' an' harder work dan she can.

"But dat bad spell of 'fluinzy [influenza] dat catch me in 1934, it just 'bout get me down. It kept me abed 'most a week, an' I ain't never rightly got over it yet. I's got a big frame, an' I used to weigh two hunnerd pounds, but dey tell me dat I only weighs a hunnert pounds now. Dis Louis Southern dat I lives wid, he de youngest son of my grandson, who was de son of my youngest daughter. An' she was born long after I was forty years old. An' dat gal was born 'fore Texas join dese here United States, just after Gen'l Sam Houston whup ol' Santy Anna. My marse, he know Gen'l Houston, an' I seed him many a time.

"I helped my young marsters get ready to fight in de Indian war an' de freedom war. I allus tell my chilluns, an' I told 'em to eat parched corn an' goobers just 'fore a fight, an' be sho to hold a crab claw in your mouth, an' you win de battle an' not get no wounds. Iffen dey gwine play ball or things like dat, I allus tells 'em not to eat no goobers just 'fore playin' 'cause dey gwine be unlucky. Dat's sho de truth 'bout a crap game. I allus tell my gals not to leave no part of no onion layin' round 'cause it sho is bad luck. An' not to have no goober hulls round de door, 'cause you goin' to jail sho.

"I don't know as I knows what you mean by snake tales, but I learn a lot about snakes. Iffen you see a wavy snake track, dat a pizen snake ain't gwine harm nobody. Did you ever fry an eel? You haven't? Well, I tells you dis for a fact, you can fry de pieces of dat ol' eel, an' you let de meat get cold, an' it'll get all raw an' bloody again. Iffen you put a piece of an eel in a fryin' pan, de foots comin' out just soon as dat meat get hot.

"Yes'm, I knows a lot 'bout de beasts. You know, a long time ago, de beasts could sho talk, an' dey carried on dey business an' dey debbilment just like folkses. Iffen you see a snake doctor [mosquito hawk], ol' man snake mighty nearby. You can beat an' beat a snake, an' de snake doctor, he come by, an' he fan an' buzz round dat snake, an' den de snake come alive again. Onliest way you can know de snake gwine stay daid is to cut off he haid. When I takes my granchillun fishin', I has to watch out for de cooter [terrapin] an' de crawfish, 'cause iffen dey gets holt of you, dey gwine hold on till it thunders. Don't never let nobody get you into killin' a turtle, 'cause he gwine come back an' haint you sho. Dem spring lizards are sho pizen. Iffen dey bite you, you gwine to die.

"Most dat I 'members 'bout church in slavery time was when de white folkses would take us to dere church. Us sat in de back of de church, an' after de big dinner on de ground, den in de afternoon, us get preached to by de white man. Some of de servants, mostly de ol' ones, would preach to us. An' den de black folks would get off down in de creek bottom or in a thicket an' sing an' shout an' pray. Don't know why, but de white folks sho didn't like dem ring shouts de colored folks had. De folks get in a ring an' sing an' dance an' shout. De dance is just a kinda shuffle, den it gets faster an' faster as dey gets warmed up, an' dey moans an' shouts an' sings an' claps an' dance. Some of 'em gets exhausted, an' dey drop out, an' de ring gets closer. Sometimes, dey sing an' shout all night, but at de break of day de nigger gotta get to de cabin an' get 'bout he business for de day. Come breakfast, old Marster, he gotta know where every one of de servants is, an' tell 'em of de tasks for de day. De white folks say de ring shout make de nigger lose he haid, an' dat he get all 'cited up an' be good for nothin' for a week.

"De Good Book is a pow'ful sign. Iffen you make you a wish an' open de Bible an' find de words 'And it shall come to pass' dere on de page, dat is de sign dat you gwine get your wish come true. I allus keep two needles crossed in de crown of my hat or in my haid rag, an' den cain't nobody work no trick on me.

"Don't know nothin' 'bout superstitions, but I knows dat ol' black Tom, he had him a jack [a mojo, or charm, swung like a pendulum in divination rituals]. It looked like a little bottle, an' he had spell roots an' water in it, an' sulphur an' I don't know what else, but he sho could find out iffen a servant gwine get a whippin'. He had a string round it, an' he just catch dis string 'tween he thumb an' finger, an' he say, 'By some Peter, by some Paul, an' by the God dat makes us all, jack, don't you tell me no lie, iffen Massa gwine whip Mary—or whoever it was—now tell me, jack!' An' sho as you're born, iffen dat jack turn to de left, den dat nigger, he get a whippin'. But iffen Marse hadn't make up he mind what he gwine do, den de jack would stand an' quiver.

"Dere sho a lot of learnin' 'bout de roots. Dey good medicine when you be sick, an' dey bring you good luck, an' dey gwine get you outen trouble iffen you smart nuff to use 'em. You white folks just go through de woods an' you don't know nothin'. Now, iffen you dig out some splinters from de north side of a big ol' pine tree what am been struck by lightnin', an' you takes dese splinters an' get 'em hot in a iron skillet, den you tech a match to 'em an' burn 'em to ashes. Den put dese ashes in a brown paper sack. Den iffen de officers get you an' you gwine have to go 'fore de judge, you just take an' get dese ashes an' get outdoors, an' at twelve o'clock at night you hold dis bag in your hand an' look up at de moon, but don't you open you mouth. Next mornin', get up early, go to de courthouse, an' sprinkle dem ashes in de doorway, an' everything dat gwine try to get in your way, an' dat law trouble, it all gwine get torn just like de lightnin' done tore dat tree.

"De shoestring root am pow'ful strong. Iffen you chew on it while you askin' for something, you gwine get it. You can get more money on a job an' just most anything iffen you chew it an' spit a ring round de person you want somethin' from. But one of de best things I knows about is a black cat bone. I had one, but since I can't see so well it got away from me.

"I was a member of de Galilee Cullud Baptist Church east of Rosebud, an' I join dat church in 1916. Den in 1921, I moved to the ridge where I is now, but I didn't bother to get no letter. I's too ol' now to work in de house or garden. An' 'sides, I can't see nohow to get round. It wears me out to talk an' bother wid folkses. Dat pension money am sho mighty fine. It ain't much, but it sho helps out. De white folks sho mighty good to me, an' I praise de Lawd for His mercy to me all de days of my life.

"Course, de slaves time to time would run 'way. Don't know iffen dey went up north or not. Didn't none on Marse place run 'way 'cause he was better to us dan de average, an' us knowed it. Course, us had to work hard, but most of de white folkses worked, an' us had plenty to eat of de ordinary run of vittles. Some things dat us had to eat den would sho be good eatin' for a millionaire now—wild turkey, bear, deer, an' such. Marse had he own white doctor when ol' Miss an' some de ol' ones couldn't touch de disease what ailed us. An' de ol' folkses just sat round an' knit or patch shoes an' harness an' such, an' dey didn't have no certain thing set for 'em to do.

"No, I never knowed of one of us runnin' away. But dere was a big whale of a black man on de plantation next ours. De overseer, he didn't like dis man nohow, an' he whup him an' he whup him. By-me-by, some white folkses, dey come travelin' through de country, an' dey hear tales 'bout how mean de overseer was to de black man. Den dey went along, an' one night, way 'bout one o'clock, us heard de hounds an' de shoutin', an' de word was whispered round dat he got 'way an' gone to find de travelers. Us all wake, but no sound in de cabins. Every nigger, he in he place. De folks hunt an' de dogs bay an' holler all through de woods de next day. But dey ain't catch dat man. He white folks, dey come our place, an' dey ask question. Don't nobody know nothin'. In a day or two, dey trail dem travelers, an' den de word come back dat de black man not wid 'em. After while, dey don't find him, an' things settle down.

" 'Bout two weeks after dat, I was in de woods huntin' berries an' gwine to fish iffen I finds a likely spot. I sat down, an' I hears a rustlin' in de bushes. I sho dat it a rabbit. After while, I feels eyes on me. De bushes, dey open a ways, an' de awfulest sight I ever hopes to see almost falls on me. Dat black man, he all tore by briars an' bit by skeeters, an' he close all 'bout gone. He cry an' begs for somethin' to eat. No'm, I didn't carry him no nothin' to eat. Come de white folks catch me doin' dat, an' it's good-bye for me.

"Yes'm, I 'spect some corn pone an' bacon get down to dat creek. No'm, it didn't 'zactly fall in de creek. De old folks say dat de black man tell 'em dat de hounds get on he track an' run him an' run him till he just 'bout drop in he tracks. Den he come 'cross a grave in de woods. An' he 'members what he granma tell him all de time. An' he gets on de left-hand side of de grave, an' quick as a wink he scratch up a handful of dat grave dirt, an' he walks backward an' scatter dis grave dirt in he tracks, an' den he toss de last speck he had over he left shoulder. Den he light out again. But de hounds, he don't hear 'em, an' he stop, listen, den slip back a piece, but dey ain't no hounds nowhere. Dey didn't bay no more.

"Yes'm, he get clear 'way. I don't 'member no more."

Endnotes

[1] Harriet Jacobs, "Incidents in the Life of a Slave Girl, Written by Herself," *Documenting the American South*, http://docsouth.unc.edu/jacobs/jacobs.html (accessed October 15, 2005).

[2] Deborah Gray White, *Aren't I a Woman: Female Slaves in the Plantation South*, rev. ed. (New York: W. W. Norton & Co., 1999), 24.

[3] Saidiya V. Hartman, *Scenes of Subjection: Terror, Slavery, and Self-Making in Nineteenth-Century America* (New York: Oxford University Press, 1997), 11.

[4] Mary Young, *All My Trials, Lord: Selections from Women's Slave Narratives* (New York: Franklin Watts, 1995), 13.

[5] Young, 14.

[6] Mary Prince, "The History of Mary Prince, a West Indian Slave. Related by Herself. With a Supplement by the Editor. To

Which Is Added, the Narrative of Asa-Asa, a Captured African," *Documenting the American South*, http://docsouth.unc.edu/neh/prince/prince.html (accessed October 15, 2005).

[7] Sojourner Truth, "The Narrative of Sojourner Truth, a Northern Slave, Emancipated from Bodily Servitude by the State of New York, in 1828," *Documenting the American South*, http://docsouth.unc.edu/neh/truth50/truth50.html (accessed October 15, 2005).

[8] Jacobs.

[9] Elizabeth Fox Genovese, *Within the Plantation Household: Black and White Women in the Old South* (Chapel Hill: University of North Carolina Press, 1988), 376.

[10] Jacobs.

[11] Ibid.

[12] Ibid.

[13] Paul D. Escott, *Slavery Remembered: A Record of Twentieth-Century Slave Narratives* (Chapel Hill: University of North Carolina Press, 1988), 2.

[14] Norman Yetman, "An Introduction to the WPA Slave Narratives," *Born in Slavery: Slave Narratives from the Federal Writers' Project, 1936-1938*, http://memory.loc.gov/ammem/snhtml/snhome.html (accessed October 24, 2005).

[5] Ibid.

[16] Norman Yetman, "Ex-Slave Interviews and the Historiography of Slavery," *American Quarterly* 36 (Summer 1984): 181-210.

[17] John Sekora, "Black Message/White Envelope: Genre, Authenticity, and Authority in the Antebellum Slave Narrative," *Callaloo* 32 (Summer 1987): 482-515.

[18] White, 24.

[19] White, 46.

[20] White, 61.

[21] Genovese, 292.

[22] Catherine Clinton, *The Plantation Mistress: Woman's World in the Old South* (New York: Pantheon Books, 1982), 201-2.

[23] Henry Louis Gates, "Not Gone With the Wind: Voices of Slavery," *New York Times*, February 9, 2003.

[24] White, 141.

[25] Sarah Sweeley, "Geneva Tonsill and the WPA Slave Narratives," *History 3090: The American South Student Projects*, http://www.arches.uga.edu/~mgagnon/students/3090/04SP3090-Sweeley.htm (accessed January 8, 2006).

26 Nieal Alden, "Sarah H. Hall and the Ex-Slave Narratives: Exploring the Validity of the WPA Georgia Writers' Project," *History 3090: The American South Student Projects*, http://www.arches.uga.edu/~mgagnon/students/3090/04SP3090-Alden.htm (accessed January 8, 2006).

27 Barbara Ehrenreich and Deirdre English, *Witches, Midwives, and Nurses: A History of Women Healers* (New York: Feminist Press at CUNY, 1972), 1.

28 Ibid.

29 Lawrence Levine, *Black Culture and Black Consciousness: Afro-American Folk Thought from Slavery to Freedom* (New York: Oxford University Press, 1978), 63.

30 Todd L. Savitt, "Slave Health and Southern Distinctiveness," in Todd L. Slavitt and James Harvey Young, eds., *Disease and Distinctiveness in the American South* (Knoxville: University of Tennessee Press, 1988), 141.

31 John S. Mbiti, *African Religions and Philosophies* (Garden City, N.Y.: Anchor Books, 1970), 141.

32 Levine, 64.

33 Sharla M. Fett, *Working Cures: Healing, Health, and Power on Southern Slave Plantations* (Chapel Hill: University of North Carolina Press, 2002), 8.

34 Ibid.

[35] Barbara Bush, "Hard Labor: Women, Childbirth, and Resistance in British Caribbean Slave Societies," in David Barry Gaspar and Darlene Clark Hine, *More Than Chattel: Black Women and Slavery in the Americas* (Bloomington: Indiana University Press, 1996), 206.

[36] Bush, 207.

[37] Levine, 74.

[38] White, 135.

[39] Lucy Stone, quoted in Steven Weisenberger, "A Historic Margaret Garner," *Margaret Garner: A New American Opera*, http://www.margaretgarner.org/AHistoricalMargaretGarner.pdf (accessed January 28, 2006).

[40] Toni Morrison, *Beloved* (New York: Knopf, 1987), 241-42.

[41] White, 105-8.

[42] Obie Clayton, Ronald B. Mincy, and David Blankenhorn, eds., *Black Fathers in Contemporary American Society: Strengths, Weaknesses, and Strategies for Change* (New York: Russell Sage Foundation: 2003).

[43] White, 110.

[44] Jacobs.

[45] June Sochen, *Herstory: A Woman's View of American History* (New York: Alfred Publishing, 1974), 4.

[46] White, 23.

[47] Peter Parish, *Slavery: The Many Faces of a Southern Institution* (Edinburgh, Scotland: Edinburgh University Press, 1995), 4-5.

[48] Jennifer L. Morgan, "State of the Field: Slavery," panel discussion, Organization of American Historians annual meeting, Boston Marriott Copley Place, March 28, 2004.

[49] Jennifer L. Morgan, *Laboring Women: Reproduction and Gender in New World Slavery* (Philadelphia: University of Pennsylvania Press, 2004), 4.

[50] Morgan, *Laboring Women*, 198.

Bibliography

Alden, Nieal. "Sarah H. Hall and the Ex-Slave Narratives: Exploring the Validity of the WPA Georgia Writers' Project." *History 3090: The American South Student Projects.* http://www.arches.uga.edu/~mgagnon/students/3090/04SP3090-Alden.htm (accessed January 8, 2006).

Bush, Barbara. "Hard Labor: Women, Childbirth, and Resistance in British Caribbean Slave Societies." In David Barry Gaspar and Darlene Clark Hine, *More Than Chattel: Black Women and Slavery in the Americas.* Bloomington: Indiana University Press, 1996.

Clayton, Obie, Ronald B. Mincy, and David Blankenhorn, eds. *Black Fathers in Contemporary American Society: Strengths, Weaknesses, and Strategies for Change.* New York: Russell Sage Foundation, 2003.

Clinton, Catherine. *The Plantation Mistress: Woman's World in the Old South.* New York: Pantheon Books, 1982.

Ehrenreich, Barbara, and Deirdre English. *Witches, Midwives, and Nurses: A History of Women Healers*. New York: Feminist Press at CUNY, 1972.

"1850 Census—South Carolina." *Census Online*. http://www.census-online.com/links/SC/1850.html (accessed January 6, 2006).

Escott, Paul D. *Slavery Remembered: A Record of Twentieth-Century Slave Narratives*. Chapel Hill: University of North Carolina Press, 1988.

Fett, Sharla M. *Working Cures: Healing, Health, and Power on Southern Slave Plantations*. Chapel Hill: University of North Carolina Press, 2002.

Fox-Genovese, Elizabeth. *Within the Plantation Household: Black and White Women in the Old South*. Chapel Hill: University of North Carolina Press, 1988.

Hartman, Saidiya V. *Scenes of Subjection: Terror, Slavery, and Self-Making in Nineteenth-Century America*. New York: Oxford University Press, 1997.

Jacobs, Harriet. "Incidents in the Life of a Slave Girl, Written by Herself." *Documenting the American South*. http://docsouth.unc.edu/jacobs/jacobs.html (accessed October 15, 2005).

Kenworthy, Sarah. "The Jim Crow South: Racial Etiquette and Its Implications in the Slave Narratives." *History 3090:*

The American South Student Projects. http://www.arches.uga.edu/ ~mgagnon/students/3090/04SP3090-Alden.htm (accessed January 22, 2006).

Levine, Lawrence. *Black Culture and Black Consciousness: Afro-American Folk Thought from Slavery to Freedom.* New York: Oxford University Press, 1978.

Mbiti, John S. *African Religions and Philosophies.* Garden City, N.Y.: Anchor Books, 1970.

Morgan, Jennifer L. *Laboring Women: Reproduction and Gender in New World Slavery.* Philadelphia: University of Pennsylvania Press, 2004.

———. "State of the Field: Slavery." Panel discussion, Organization of American Historians annual meeting, Boston Marriott Copley Place, March 28, 2004.

Morrison, Toni. *Beloved.* New York: Knopf, 1987.

Parish, Peter. *Slavery: The Many Faces of a Southern Institution.* Edinburgh, Scotland: Edinburgh University Press, 1995.

Prince, Mary. "The History of Mary Prince, a West Indian Slave. Related by Herself. With a Supplement by the Editor. To Which Is Added, the Narrative of Asa-Asa, a Captured African." *Documenting the American South.* http://docsouth.unc.edu/neh/prince/ prince.html (accessed October 15, 2005).

Rawick, George P., ed. *The American Slave: A Composite Auto-biography*. 19 vols. Westport, Conn.: Greenwood Publishing Co., 1972. Greenwood Electronic Media offers this work online by subscription at http://www.gem.greenwood.com/products/prod_amslav.asp.

Savitt, Todd L. "Slave Health and Southern Distinctiveness." In Todd L. Savitt and James Harvey Young, eds., *Disease and Distinctiveness in the American South*. Knoxville: University of Tennessee Press, 1988.

Sekora, John. "Black Message/White Envelope: Genre, Authenticity, and Authority in the Antebellum Slave Narrative." *Callaloo* 32 (Summer 1987): 482-515.

Sochen, June. *Herstory: A Woman's View of American History*. New York: Alfred Publishing, 1974.

Sweeley, Sarah. "Geneva Tonsill and the WPA Slave Narratives." *History 3090: The American South Student Projects*. http://www.arches.uga.edu/~mgagnon/students/3090/04SP3090-Sweeley.htm (accessed January 8, 2006).

Truth, Sojourner. "The Narrative of Sojourner Truth, a Northern Slave, Emancipated from Bodily Servitude by the State of New York, in 1828." *Documenting the American South*. http://docsouth.unc.edu/neh/truth50/truth50.html (accessed October 15, 2005).

Weisenberger, Steven. "A Historic Margaret Garner." *Margaret Garner: A New American Opera*. http://www.margaretgarner.org/AHistoricalMargaretGarner.pdf (accessed January 28, 2006).

White, Deborah Gray. *Ar'n't I a Woman: Female Slaves in the Plantation South*. Rev. ed. New York: W. W. Norton & Co., 1999.

Yetman, Norman. "Ex-Slave Interviews and the Historiography of Slavery." *American Quarterly* 36 (Summer 1984): 181-210.

———. "An Introduction to the WPA Slave Narratives." *Born in Slavery: Slave Narratives from the Federal Writers' Project, 1936-1938*. http://memory.loc.gov/ammem/snhtml/snhome.html (accessed October 24, 2005).

Young, Mary. *All My Trials, Lord: Selections from Women's Slave Narratives*. New York: Franklin Watts, 1995.